PRAISE FOR

NEW TESTAMENT SURVEY I

"This is a valuable resource for both students and devotional readers alike. Lemaster's approach is refreshing—clear and detailed, offering depth without losing the reader in minutiae. Each section is structured thoughtfully, providing a well-organized and accessible framework for understanding the New Testament. What stands out most is Lemaster's ability to convey the authorial intent of each book in a way that is both insightful and easy to grasp, making this volume a remarkable tool for those looking to deepen their comprehension of Scripture with precision. This survey is an ideal guide for academic studies and personal devotional use."

— Dr. Mark Zhakevich, Associate Professor of New Testament
Chairman, New Testament Department, The Master's Seminary

"In this volume Nathan LeMaster provides the reader with a succinct but not simplistic survey of the synoptic gospels—Matthew, Mark and Luke—the book of Acts and all of the Johannine literature in the New Testament (Gospel of John, the three Epistles of John and Revelation). The Introduction contains a brief but very helpful historical and textual background of the New Testament. Since each New Testament book is surveyed as to structure, purpose, and themes, the reader is not only provided with a clear idea of the contents of each book, but a reference guide for comparison and analysis of the biblical theology of each book. The various "themes" highlighted in each chapter become a virtual "mini-biblical theology"; these themes are presented concisely and yet the reader will have a good grasp of the place and importance of each "theme" in the book being surveyed. Dr. LeMaster deals with the complex issues of chronology (e.g. as pertaining related to the life of Jesus) with succinct clarity, and he addresses a number of controversial issues in biblical theology (e.g., in his treatment of the biblical theology of the Book of the Revelation) without "getting lost in the weeds" of controversy. This book is well written and will be an exceptionally helpful book for all students of the Bible at all levels."

— Dr. Kevin D. Zuber, Professor of Theology
Chairman, Theology Department, The Master's Seminary

Titles in the Christian Life Series

Published in 2023

Heaven and Hell: A Survey of the Biblical Doctrines of Personal Eschatology (Kevin Zuber)

The Forgotten Attributes of God: God's Nature and Why It Matters (Peter Sammons)

Old Testament Survey I: Genesis to Esther (Nathan LeMaster)

Well Done: A Strategy for Life Stewardship (Reagan Rose)

Becoming a Worthy Reader: How to Read and Study the Bible (Kevin Zuber)

Published in 2024

New Testament Survey I: Matthew to Acts & Johannine Literature (Nathan LeMaster)

Gender and Sexuality (Michael Riccardi)

Coming in 2025 (tentative titles)

The Church and Church Membership (John MacArthur)

Old Testament Survey II (Nathan LeMaster)

Salvation and Sanctification (author TBD)

The Spiritual Disciplines (author TBD)

Coming in 2026 and beyond (tentative titles)

Spiritual Leadership (author TBD)

The Creeds of the Church (author TBD)

New Testament Survey II (Nathan LeMaster)

Spiritual Gifts and Service (author TBD)

The Person of God or *The Authority of Scripture* (author TBD)

Biblical Reconciliation (author TBD)

Marriage and Family Counseling (author TBD)

Discipling and Mentoring (author TBD)

Global and Local Missions (author TBD)

BIBLE KNOWLEDGE

New Testament Survey I

Matthew to Acts & Johannine Literature

NATHAN LEMASTER

CLC PUBLICATIONS
Fort Washington, PA 19034

New Testament Survey I: Matthew to Acts and Johannine Literature
The Christian Life Series

Published by CLC Publications

USA: P.O. Box 1449, Fort Washington, PA 19034
www.clcpublications.com

UK: Kingsway CLC Trust
Unit 5, Glendale Avenue, Sandycroft, Flintshire, CH5 2QP
www.equippingthechurch.com

ISBN (paperback): 978-1-61958-394-8
ISBN (ebook): 978-1-61958-396-2

Printed in the United States of America

Italics in Scripture quotations, if not original to the NASB, are the emphasis of the author.

Contents

Series Foreword

The Christian Life Series

From the time the Lord called me to Grace Community Church, I have had two primary goals: to preach the Word of God faithfully (2 Tim. 4:2) and to entrust the truth to faithful men (2:2). In keeping with those priorities, The Master's Seminary has played a key role in training future pastors to handle the Word accurately and defend its truth boldly. These Master's men have gone out to serve and shepherd churches across the nation and around the world.

Several years ago, to assist these faithful pastors in their shepherding work, the seminary created a lay-training program, comprised of online video courses. The Institute for the Christian Life is designed to train lay people in four fundamental categories: Bible Knowledge, Sound Doctrine, Christian Living, and Shepherding Care, bringing biblical training, theological instruction, and practical ministry into the pew and the living room—making these indispensable tools accessible to believers at all levels of spiritual maturity and church leadership. This book series complements those online courses, as an aid for small group discussion and individual study.

My prayer for you as you read this book is that you would grow in the grace and knowledge of the Lord Jesus Christ. As the apostle Paul expressed in Ephesians 1:18–19, "*I pray* that the eyes of your heart may be enlightened, so that you will know what is the hope of His calling, what are the riches of the glory of His inheritance in the saints, and what is the surpassing greatness of His power toward us who believe."

John MacArthur
Pastor, Grace Community Church, Sun Valley, California
Chancellor, The Master's University and Seminary

Editorial Preface

Dr. Nathan LeMaster (PhD, Cambridge) serves as Assistant Professor of Old Testament at The Master's Seminary. He presents the second volume in a series of introductory works dedicated to Bible Survey; this volume places an unwavering focus on the New Testament, a testament that unveils the profound teachings of our Savior.

In the resounding wisdom of Martin Luther, "Let the man who would hear God speak, read Holy Scriptures." This timeless directive underscores the profound significance of delving into the sacred texts, particularly the revelation encapsulated in the New Testament through the life and light emanating from Jesus Christ. In the pages of the New Testament, a divine tapestry unfolds, weaving together the transformative narrative of Christ's teachings, life, and redemptive mission. As we heed Luther's counsel and immerse ourselves in the Holy Scriptures, the New Testament unfolds as a source of eternal wisdom, ushering us into the transformative brilliance of God's eternal plan for us.

This transformative volume delves into the timeless narratives of the Synoptic Gospels, the dynamic history of the book of Acts, and the illuminating wisdom of Johannine literature. It is a wonderful overview, chapter by chapter, unveiling the profound themes and pivotal events in the books of Matthew through Acts, alongside the insightful epistles of John.

Whether you stand as a seasoned minister with time-tested experience or find yourself newly embraced by the divine truth, we anticipate that this book will not only provide the scholarly rigor you seek but also offer a refreshing wellspring to invigorate your personal study. May it be a guiding light in your journey, aiding you in your labor for the Lord with renewed zeal and profound insights from the New Testament.

Peter Sammons, PhD, Series Editor
Author of *Reprobation and God's Sovereignty*
and *The Forgotten Attributes of God*

Introduction

THOSE WHO COME TO study the New Testament must ask themselves a simple question: "Is the New Testament reliable?" If the New Testament speaks the truth, then it turns our whole world upside down. I, personally, have never seen a blind man healed of his blindness. I have never seen someone raised from the dead. I have never seen Jesus. But Matthew has. John has. Peter has. The testimony of these eyewitnesses is crucial. The New Testament begins with the Gospels for an important reason: Jesus is the central focus of the New Testament, from Matthew to Revelation. To study the New Testament is to study who Jesus was and is. The New Testament, as the Word of God, reminds us that our world is a very small part of God's work in the world.

The New Testament also exults the Christian beyond anything that we know. Paul expresses the foundational truths of what it means to be a Christian in Romans. Eternal life is a phrase that we do not understand. John tries to explain his vision of what heaven will be like, but it is not possible to fully grasp this until, by faith, we arrive. The New Testament is a window into the glorious reality which is awaiting the Christian: Life with Christ. The New Testament is also the guidebook for the church for this age while we wait for that glorious return of Christ.

The Organization of the New Testament

Just as with the Old Testament, it is important to understand the organization of the New Testament. Of course, the New Testament begins with the Gospels, but Matthew is placed first for an important reason. Matthew, as will be seen in its own chapter, perfectly links together the Old Testament with the New.

In addition, it is also important to recognize that there are four Gospels, each one having a unique argument and focus. The Gospels are not contradictory but complementary. Together they demonstrate what God has communicated to us through His Son. Also, Acts is not just a history book, but a second volume written by Luke, meant to be studied together with the Gospel of Luke. For this reason, this first survey volume of the New Testament will examine Luke and Acts consecutively.

The Pauline letters come after Acts, generally organized not according to when they were written but by size, from the longest to the shortest. This is Romans through Philemon. The non-Pauline letters come after this also, generally organized from largest to smallest, starting with Hebrews and going to Jude. Letters written to the same church or person are kept together such as First and Second Thessalonians and First and Second Timothy.

Because this first survey volume deals with the Gospel of John, all of the writings of John will be addressed in this first volume. Therefore, Matthew, Mark, Luke, Acts, John, First John, Second John, Third John, and Revelation will comprise our chapters. However, before we delve into these chapters we must first do some background study. It is important, when making the leap from the Old Testament to the New Testament, to understand the Second Temple Period, which spans for more than four centuries. No books of the Bible were written from the time between Malachi and Matthew, but a great deal changed in the landscape of history over that time. In addition, it will also be important to discuss the historicity of the New Testament, along with a survey of the manuscripts which we have for the New Testament. This is not meant to be a data dump, but I do want to help you see how we have come to have the New Testament today. What are the manuscripts and how do we know they haven't been altered over the course of 2,000 years?

Additionally, we want to take a look at the relationship of the New Testament and the Old Testament. How did the New Testament authors make use of the Old Testament? Are there any contradictions or claims that the Old Testament authors misunderstood God's promises? How the New Testament authors used the Old Testament is a guide for us when we seek to properly understand the New Testament.

The Second Temple Period

The Second Temple Period derives its name from the temple which was built by those Jews who returned from exile under the leadership of Zerubbabel. This temple was completed in 515 BC and stood on the site of the temple built by Solomon which was destroyed in the Babylonian invasion.[1] From

1 For an excellent breakdown of the Second Temple Period, see Andreas J. Köstenberger, Charles L Quarles, and L. Scott Kellum, *The Cradle, the Cross, and the Crown* (Nashville: B&H Academic, 2009): 58–99.

515 BC until AD 70 is referred to as the Second Temple Period, AD 70 being the destruction of this temple originally built by Zerubbabel. The following is a breakdown of the time periods which are in this Second Temple Period:

1. Babylonian Period: 606–539 BC
2. Persian Period: 539–331 BC
3. Greek Period: 331–167 BC
   a. Alexander the Great: 331–320 BC
   b. Ptolemaic Period: 320–198 BC
   c. Syrian Period: 198–167 BC
4. Jewish Self-Rule: 167–63 BC
   a. Maccabean Period: 167–142 BC
   b. Hasmonean Period: 142–63 BC
5. Roman Period: 63 BC–AD 70[2]

A great deal of the Old Testament speaks to the Babylonian Period. Israel was split into two kingdoms right after the death of King Solomon, c. 930 BC. From 930 BC until 722 BC the northern kingdom of Israel and the southern kingdom of Judah were separated and often at war with each other. In 722 BC Israel was conquered by Assyria. While Israel had several dynasties during this period, Judah continued to have a descendent of David on the throne all the way until Babylon finally destroyed Judah and Jerusalem in 586 BC. But Nebuchadnezzar II, the supreme ruler of Babylonia, first invaded Judah in 606 BC, establishing his dominion in the area. Once Jerusalem was destroyed, along with the temple, the Jewish people were sent into exile to Babylonia. It was actually at this time that the first synagogues were built, compensating for the fact that the temple had been destroyed.

Nebuchadnezzar II was a powerful ruler, but his successors failed to maintain the same power and prestige. Four successors came after Nebuchadnezzar II, the last being Nabonidus, who ruled from 556 to 539 BC. Belshazzar (Dan. 5) was a co-ruler alongside Nabonidus. In 539 BC, Babylon was captured suddenly and unexpectedly by Cyrus the Great, a Persian. This began the Persian Empire, also known as the Achaemenid Empire, which ruled from 539 to 331 BC.

It was during this Persian Period that the Jews were allowed to return to Jerusalem. Jeremiah 29:10 prophesies this return: "For thus says the Lord,

2 Köstenberger, Quarles, and Kellum, 59.

'When seventy years have been completed for Babylon, I will visit you and fulfill My good word to you, to bring you back to this place.'" It was Cyrus the Great who issued the decree that the Jews may return to their homeland. This return to Jerusalem and the surrounding region was accomplished over several years with several waves of returning exiles. In 515 BC Zerubbabel dedicated the newly built temple. Ezra 3:12–13 states:

> Yet many of the priests and Levites and heads of fathers' *households*, the old men who had seen the first temple, wept with a loud voice when the foundation of this house was laid before their eyes, while many shouted aloud for joy, so that the people could not distinguish the sound of the shout of joy from the sound of the weeping of the people.

From 515 to 400 BC there were a few prophets who spoke in the name of the Lord: Haggai, Zechariah, and Malachi. After 400 BC God sent no more prophets to Jerusalem. However, Malachi, the last of the Old Testament prophets, pointed to the future coming of John the Baptist (Malachi 4:5). The next revelation to be given will be a little baby, born in Bethlehem and placed in a manger.

The Persian Empire was thrown into chaos when a young general by the name of Alexander went on the warpath. Alexander the Great struck a major blow against the Persian Empire in 333 BC at the battles of Granicus and Issus, defeating Darius II at Arbela in 331 BC and bringing an end to the Persian Empire.[3] Alexander the Great continued to extend his military reach but also his cultural reach as well. The more that Alexander conquered, the more the Greek language and culture were spread over the known world. However, Alexander's triumph was short-lived; he died in 323 BC with no heir. His generals began fighting for control of the empire, eventually dividing the empire into four: The Ptolemaic Kingdom in Egypt, the Seleucid Kingdom in the eastern portion of the empire, the Pergamon Kingdom in Asia Minor, and the Macedonian Kingdom. The Ptolemaic and Seleucid Kingdoms fought for control of Israel.

In 320 BC, the Ptolemaic Kingdom gained control of Israel and ruled it from Egypt for more than one hundred years. During that time the Septuagint (the Greek translation of the Hebrew Old Testament), was completed, having been translated over a lengthy period. This became the standard translation of the Old Testament, since Hebrew was dying out as a language at this time, even before the return of the exiles from Babylon.

---

3 Köstenberger, Quarles, and Kellum, 60.

In 198 BC Antiochus III defeated Ptolemy V, giving the Seleucid Kingdom control over Israel.[4] It was the infamous Antiochus IV (known by the title Epiphanes, which means "Glorious One"), who invaded Jerusalem in 168 BC, sacrificing a pig on the altar and desecrating the temple. The outcry against the Seleucids was great, and the priest Mattathias began a revolt against the Seleucids. This rebellion did not end quickly; Mattathias' sons (who became known as the Maccabees) carried on the rebellion after him. Judas (164–161 BC), Jonathan (161–142 BC), and Simon (142–135 BC) each led the revolt at different times. During Simon's leadership, Israel gained its independence from the Seleucids, only to be reconquered later. Simon was assassinated by his son-in-law, along with two of his sons. A third son, John Hyrcanus I, became the de facto leader of the people, even though he did not have the title "king."

The Maccabees were priests, as seen with Mattathias. Some of them attained the title of "king" though only for a while. John Hyrcanus was viewed as a priest and ruler, but not as king. This became a sticking point later on. The Maccabean family established the Hasmonean Dynasty, the word "Hasmonean" supposedly coming from one of their ancestors. Ruling power waned and waxed as the Hasmoneans continued to battle for control against the Seleucids as well as other waring factions and kingdoms in the area. Aristobulus I took over for his father John Hyrcanus, ruling for only a year. Alexander Janneus then took power, ruling from 103 to 76 BC. Salome Alexandra then ruled from 76 to 67 BC, and Aristobulus II ruled from 67 to 63 BC.

It was at this time that the Roman might swept over Jerusalem. There was constant in-fighting among the Hasmoneans, and the Roman general Pompey capitalized on this after defeating the Seleucid Kingdom. Pompey besieged and captured Jerusalem through both military might and political maneuvering. The year was 63 BC, and Rome would rule Judea from that point on, eventually destroying the temple in AD 70.

The Hasmoneans still maintained some form of power, mostly as priests, though they were deprived of political power. In the throes of the end of the Roman republic, Herod was named king of Judea by the Roman senate. Herod, though he did not come from the Hasmonean line nor from any royal line, gained power through political maneuvering with the Romans. Herod was named king of Judea in 40 BC.

Herod had the support of Rome, but not necessarily the support of his own people. Herod had the ability to maneuver himself politically to avoid destruction, but his political maneuvering caused the people to view him

4 Köstenberger, Quarles, and Kellum, 61.

more as a power grabber than as a true Jewish ruler. In addition, Herod was not from the Hasmonean line. The Hasmoneans constantly fought and struggled for power, but once Herod came to power, the people were quick to point out that he was not in the Hasmonean line. Herod was not a usurper in the traditional sense, but he was also not viewed as being entirely legitimate by the people. In order to appease the people, Herod undertook a major building project: an expansion of the temple.

By the time Herod had completed the work on the temple, it was considered one of the eight wonders of the ancient world.[5] Herod also undertook major building projects for himself, including the port at Caesarea, Masada, and Herodium. These impressive projects served to display his grandeur and wealth, but they also served as places of refuge. Herod was notoriously paranoid, and he built fortresses all over Israel so that he would always be close to a fortress should a rebellion arise.

Herod also married a Hasmonean princess, Mariamne, possibly as an attempt to authenticate his rule in the eyes of his opponents. Mariamne bore Herod many children, both sons and daughters. The extent of Herod's paranoia became obvious when he had several of his sons executed, fearing that they were trying to usurp his throne. Eventually he also had Mariamne executed for the same reason. Herod's order to execute the infants in Bethlehem (Matt. 2:16–18), for fear of a newly born king, was exactly in keeping with his character. After Herod's death, three of his remaining sons were given ruling power. Archelaus was appointed ruler over Judea, including Jerusalem, but was deposed by Rome in AD 6. (History records that he was as cruel as his father, but without the administrative skill.) Instead of appointing another Herodian ruler, Rome instead supplied governors to rule this area, the most famous being Pontius Pilate.

Philip, another of Herod's sons, was given rule in the region northeast of Galilee. Herod Antipas ruled Galilee itself. This was the Herod Antipas whom John the Baptist condemned for divorcing his wife in order to marry the wife of his half-brother (Mark 6:14–29). Both Philip and Herod Antipas played a small role in the New Testament. It is the Roman gubernatorial system which is center stage for the arrest and trial of Jesus.

Pontius Pilate was the governor at the time of Jesus' trial. He was appointed in AD 26 and was deposed as governor shortly after the time of Jesus (AD 36). Pilate was the fifth of twelve governors to rule this area from AD 6 to AD 66, at which time the Jewish rebellion began. The governors did not

---

5 Köstenberger, Quarles, and Kellum, 74.

reside in Jerusalem, but in Caesarea on the Mediterranean coast. However, a strong miliary presence was always in Jerusalem to quell any rebellion.

The Jews did have a voice in their governance. The governors allowed a ruling body, the Sanhedrin, to have authority over many areas. The Sanhedrin included many Sadducees and Pharisees, and was overseen by the high priest, which at this point was more of a political role than a religious one.

This set the stage for Jesus' arrival on the scene. Jesus was born into a tumultuous time, with many varied groups vying for power. It was a time of brutality, deceit, and violence. The Jewish people had a complex relationship with their rulers. We are able to see the trickery that the Pharisees employed against Jesus by asking Him whether they should pay taxes to Caesar. We can also see the brutality of the Roman system, nailing convicted criminals to a cross to be put on display as a sign for anyone who was considering going against Rome. Jesus arrived on the scene and spoke the truth about God. He spoke about the kingdom of heaven and the blessedness of those who are meek. Jesus pointed to the heart of the Mosaic law by saying that anger breaks the commandment against murder, and lust breaks the commandment against adultery. This was an age when the rulers of the land were not only committing adultery on a regular basis, but even killed their family members because of paranoia and a mad grasp for power. Jesus pointed to the heart of the gospel and God's love for His children. Jesus said that if anyone wants to enter the kingdom of heaven, they must become like little children. This could not have stood in starker contrast to the greed, brutality, and wickedness of the times.

The Historicity of the New Testament

In addition to surveying the Second Temple Period, it is also important to look at the historicity of the New Testament. How can we trust the New Testament if it was written 2,000 years ago? Is it still accurate and reliable as a witness of the life of Jesus and the ministry of the early church? We will examine the texts and history of the transmission of the New Testament, as well as generally look at canonicity. In other words, how do we know that the books which make up the New Testament are indeed those which should be in the New Testament?[6]

---

6 There are several books which speak to these questions. One that is easy to read is the work by Amy Anderson and Wendy Widder, *Textual Criticism of the Bible* (Bellingham, WA: Lexham Press, 2018). This includes more detail about New Testament texts and textual transmission than I provide in this survey.

When looking at the history of the New Testament, we start with the writing of the individual books themselves. This was completed within the first century, even by AD 85–90. The earliest books are some of Paul's letters, written only a couple of decades after the time of Jesus. By AD 180 Iranaeus, an early church father, gives reference to the *tetraeuangelion*, the collection of the four Gospels, which are regarded as each being equally authoritative. There is also a reference in Colossians 4:16 to the spread of Paul's letters among the churches. Even though a letter may have been written to a single church, it was dispersed and read among the other churches. As the works of the New Testament were being written, the early church was receiving them, verifying the authorship and attesting to their authority. The early church fathers attested to many of the New Testament books. Such is the case with the first letter of Clement, written around AD 96, which speaks of Romans as well as First Corinthians and Hebrews. This letter from Clement was sent from Rome to Corinth and speaks to the wide acceptance of these letters of Paul.

Not only were copies being made of the writing of the New Testament and being passed from church to church, but the early church fathers also quote the New Testament in their own writings. This is done to such an extent that it is possible to recreate virtually all of the New Testament just from quotations by the early church fathers. The early church fathers wrote in Greek as well as Latin. And the New Testament, after it was compiled, was quickly translated into other languages. The Latin Vulgate was translated in the fourth century. The Syriac New Testament was completed around AD 300. There is a Coptic version of the New Testament from the third century. In the fourth, fifth, and sixth centuries Armenian, Georgian, Ethiopic, Gothic, and Slavonic translations were also made.

The question that often arises is, what are the earliest New Testament manuscripts that still exist today? Of course, we do not have any of the original manuscripts of the New Testament. Everything that exists today is a copy. There are small portions of the New Testament still in existence which date to the first half of the second century AD. However, these are small parts of the New Testament books. It was not until the 1800s that much earlier complete manuscripts of the New Testament were discovered.

Several existing complete New Testaments date to the fourth century. *Codex Sinaiticus* is one of those. It was discovered in St. Catherine's monastery at the foot of Mt. Sinai in 1859. It has been dated between AD 330 and 350. *Codex Vaticanus*, housed at the Vatican in Rome, is dated to around the same time as *Sinaiticus*. *Codex Alexandrinus* made its way from Alexandria, Egypt (where it was compiled) to Constantinople and then to England in the 17th century. It dates from the fifth century AD. Another text, *Ephraemi Rescriptus*, was discovered in 1840 and dates to the fifth century. *Codex Bezae Cantabrigiensis*, a partial text of the New Testament which contains most of the Gospels and Acts, is dated to the fifth century. But these are still copies, and any time there is a copy, errors can creep into the text. It is the original manuscripts, which no longer exist, which were inspired by the Holy Spirit. The existing manuscripts are an accurate reflection of those original documents, but that does not mean that they are perfect. By examining the data of the existing manuscripts, scholars are able to determine where errors possibly crept into the text through scribal mistakes.

It is the work of textual criticism to examine the data to uncover the original, correct reading. Of the texts which exist today, very few variants exist among the manuscripts which would change theology. The vast majority of scribal errors were misspellings and things of that sort. One of the most important textual issues is the ending of the Gospel of Mark.

Most Bible translations will put Mark 16:9–20 in brackets with the explanation that many early manuscripts do not contain these verses. This is a critical issue because Mark 16:9–20 contains some interesting statements about what God will do for Christians. Acts 16:17–18 puts the following words in the mouth of Jesus:

> These signs will accompany those who have believed: in My name they will cast out demons, they will speak with new tongues; they will pick up serpents, and if they drink any deadly *poison*, it will not hurt them; they will lay hands on the sick, and they will recover.

Many of these things can be seen in the early church. Casting out demons occurs in Acts along with healing of the sick. The reference to picking up serpents may be related to Paul on the island of Malta when he is bitten by a venomous snake but does not die (Acts 28:1–6). There are no examples of a Christian drinking poison in Acts. Unfortunately, snake handling in a few churches in America has had tragic results. But is this part of the original writing of Mark? If not, where did these verses come from? To help answer these questions we need to look at the textual evidence for the ending of Mark. Looking at the data, we see that neither *Codex Vaticanus* nor *Codex Sinaiticus* contain this ending, instead ending the Gospel of Mark at verse 8.

Additionally, the early church attests that the longer ending of Mark was not original. The external evidence, both the existing texts and the early church witness, points to the fact that this longer ending was added later. This is not to say that Vaticanus and Sinaiticus are the final word on what is correct or not. Vaticanus and Sinaiticus have discrepancies between them because they are copies, not the original text. But the agreement of the earliest texts lends support to what the original reading would have been.

Additionally, the internal evidence in Mark points to the ending being at verse 8. As will be discussed in the chapter on Mark, this Gospel is characteristically emphatic and short. To end Mark at 16:8 is abrupt, but that is keeping in line with what Mark has been doing throughout his Gospel. Ending Mark here means that there is not a resurrection appearance by Jesus. Mary Magdalene and Mary the mother of James and Salome went to the tomb of Jesus and saw that the stone had been rolled away from the tomb. Upon entering the tomb they saw an angel who told them that Jesus had risen from the dead. The angel commands the women to go and tell the disciples, and they leave the tomb gripped with fear. This abrupt ending gives no details of Jesus' appearing to the disciples. It does not mention Jesus' conversation with the two disciples on the road to Emmaus. It does not mention Jesus' conversation with Peter on the shore of Galilee. It simply ends the book and compels us to be the ones to carry on the story, spreading the good news of Jesus to the world. Perhaps it was because the ending feels so abrupt that the addition was made to the end of Mark.

We have received the entire New Testament from copies made in church history. No original manuscripts exist that we know of. But that does not mean that we are not able to see what was written. Because so many copies exist, both complete New Testaments such as the ones mentioned above as well as thousands of smaller portions of the books, we are able to trace back the data. The data which is available to us demonstrates when there was a mistake or error made by a scribe. The errors which have crept into the existing copies which would affect our understanding of doctrine are very few, only a handful of examples. On the whole the variants which exist are due to simple mistakes or copyist's errors which can be identified. We are able to see what Paul wrote to the churches, what John wrote concerning his revelation, what the Gospel writers intended to say about Jesus of Nazareth. More than any other historical document of the ancient world, we can have confidence that we know what the New Testament authors wrote.

The New Testament Use of the Old Testament

Finally, it is important to understand the New Testament use of the Old Testament. Even the terminology "Old Testament" and "New Testament" seems to imply discontinuity between the two. However, the New Testament writers did not see contradiction between what they were communicating and what the Old Testament had to say. Paul, as an example, grew up immersed in the writings of Moses and the Old Testament authors. After his conversion, Paul argued that Jesus was what the Old Testament was looking toward. As Paul uses quotations and allusions from the Old Testament, it is obvious that he is relying on it, not attempting to undermine it.

Matthew is another key example of the relationship between the two testaments. Matthew begins his Gospel with the phrase "The record of the genealogy of Jesus the Messiah, the son of David, the son of Abraham." To someone who had not studied the Old Testament, this would not make sense. Even the term Christ would not make sense. Christ is the Anointed One, the Messiah. The concept of Messiah is rooted in the Old Testament, finding its definition there. Matthew does not try to define it for his readers because he is relying on the fact that his readers know the Old Testament. Additionally, Matthew uses the term "son of David." This is rooted in the Old Testament, pointing to the promise which God made David in Second Samuel 7. By saying "son of David," Matthew is pointing to Jesus' everlasting kingship, a concept which has its foundation in the Old Testament.

Not only do the New Testament authors draw on Old Testament imagery and ideas, but they base their theological arguments in the Old Testament. Romans is a key example of this. Oftentimes, we think of Romans as being a New Testament theological treatise. Upon examining the letter, we see that Paul relies heavily upon the Old Testament. In fact, without the Old Testament as a foundation, Paul's arguments would not work. Paul uses Psalm 51 to prove his point about God's just judgment. He uses Psalms 14 and 53 to prove his point about all people being sinful. He uses Psalm 32 to argue for salvation from God as based on grace. He uses Genesis 15:6 to prove that salvation is based on faith. On and on it goes throughout all Romans and throughout the entire New Testament.

No New Testament author takes an Old Testament quotation out of context. Any time that a New Testament author makes use of the Old Testament, it is intentional, incorporating in even the context of the Old Testament passage. New Testament authors may be using Old Testament quotes in various ways, as illustration, argumentation, or proof. But no New Testament author reinterprets an Old Testament passage, making it mean something that it did not originally mean. They keep the Old Testament author's intention as they use the passage.

This helps us to understand how the New Testament authors expect to be understood. Just as they did with those who wrote before them, they expected us to understand their intention, not to go beyond that intention. Therefore, we must be careful and diligent to understand each author's intention when studying the New Testament. The passage cannot mean more than the original author intended it to mean.

Study Questions:

1. Who were the Maccabees? How do they relate to the Hasmoneans?
2. How did the Romans gain control of Israel?
3. Who was Herod and what were his great building projects? How does the story of the murder of the babies of Bethlehem fit Herod's characteristics?
4. What are the key New Testament manuscripts that are still in existence today? How reliable are the manuscripts that we have for the New Testament? Is the New Testament a historically reliable document?
5. What are the principles of interpreting the New Testament that we can learn from how the New Testament authors used the Old Testament?

PART ONE

Synoptic Gospels and Acts

1

Matthew

THE AUTHORSHIP OF Matthew is attested by the early church. Matthew nowhere actually attributes the Gospel to himself, even though he is included in several of the narratives. The title "According to Matthew" was probably attached to the Gospel as early as AD 125.[1] The dating of Matthew can also prove difficult, since no claim is made of the time of the writing in the Gospel. Many scholars disagree on the dating of Matthew, Mark, and Luke. This author holds that the best date of Matthew would be before AD 62.[2]

It can be difficult to narrow down to whom each of the Gospels was written. Luke records that he is writing to someone named "Theophilus" (to be discussed in the chapter on Luke). But Matthew makes no such claim. It must be discerned from the characteristics of the book itself as to who was Matthew's intended audience. The fact that Matthew begins with the genealogy of Jesus points to Matthew's dependence upon the Old Testament and the fact that his readers would have known the Old Testament. This idea will be further developed in the section on genealogy in this chapter.

Matthew assumes that his readers know at least a little Aramaic. In Matthew 5:22 he uses an Aramaic term without giving a Greek translation for it. The specific term for the temple treasury is also used in Matthew 27:6 and it is left unexplained, as though the reader should know what it is. Matthew also does not spend a great deal of time explaining the Jewish background,

---

1 See Donald Guthrie, *New Testament Introduction*, 4th edition (Downers Grove, IL: IVP Academic, 1990): 43–44. Guthrie is a very helpful in-depth New Testament introduction, and he gives an excellent summation of the testimony of the early church to the authorship of Matthew on pages 43–49. Several early church fathers attest to the fact that the apostle Matthew wrote the Gospel by his name. This includes Papias, Irenaeus, Pantaenus, and Origen.

2 For a full discussion on the issue of the date of Matthew see Guthrie, 53–56.

such as the Jewish rulers at the time (Matt. 2:1, 22) or Jewish customs (Matthew 15:2). The assumption of Matthew upon his readers seems to indicate that he was writing with a Jewish audience in mind, the main point of his Gospel being to show that Jesus is the Messiah.

There is some debate about which language Matthew originally wrote his Gospel. There is some evidence from the early church that Matthew first wrote his Gospel in Aramaic, and it was subsequently translated to Greek.[3] This debate is still ongoing, with scholars examining the Greek itself, which doesn't appear to be a translation, as well as examining the historical evidence. At this point, there is no consensus as to whether Matthew first wrote his Gospel in Greek or in Aramaic.

Structure

The structure of this Gospel demonstrates Matthew's focus. Matthew certainly highlights the kingship of the Messiah, so one can view the book as being structured around this idea. The breakdown would then be:

I. The King's birth (1–2)
II. The King's presentation (3–7)
III. The King's authority (8–10)
IV. The Opposition to the King (11–13)
V. The Compassion of the King (14–18)
VI. The Rejection of the King (19–25)
VII. The Death and Resurrection of the King (26–28)

As will be discussed later, the hinge point of the book is the manifested opposition to Jesus. A major shift occurs in Matthew 12–13, which paves the way for the ultimate rejection of the Messiah and subsequent death and resurrection of Jesus.

Purpose

The placement of Matthew as the first book of the New Testament is strategic. This will be discussed more in the section on genealogies. Matthew is picking up right where the Old Testament left off. Matthew places great weight on the Old Testament prophecies that speak of the coming Messiah. Matthew points to Isaiah 7:14 being fulfilled by Jesus' birth. Micah

3 For further discussion on this, see Köstenberger, Quarles, and Kellum, 182–183.

5:2 is fulfilled by the wise men in Matthew 2:6. Hosea 11:1 is fulfilled in Jesus going down into Egypt in Matthew 2:15. Jeremiah 31:15 is fulfilled in Matthew 2:18 with the slaughter of the children of Bethlehem. Matthew 3:3 says that John the Baptist fulfilled Isaiah's prophecy of being the forerunner of the Messiah. Matthew 4:14 says that Jesus' moving and settling in the Galilee region fulfilled Isaiah 9:1. Isaiah 53:4 is fulfilled in Matthew 8:17 by Jesus' healing of the sick. Jesus also fulfills Isaiah 42:1 in Matthew 12:15–18. These are only a few examples of Matthew's emphasis on the Old Testament prophecies being fulfilled by Jesus' life. All this points to Jesus who is the long-awaited Messiah and King of Israel.

> **Matthew Purpose Statement:** Matthew's purpose is to reveal Jesus as the long-expected Messiah and Davidic King of Israel.

Themes

Several themes can be seen coming out of this purpose statement. Jesus, as the Messiah and King, fulfills many roles. He is descended from king David, traced through the genealogies. He is the authority over the Mosaic Law and the fulfillment of it. He is the perfect King and inaugurates important aspects of the kingdom of heaven. And Jesus is also the Teacher of Israel. Matthew emphasizes each of these aspects by uniquely curating the content that is in his Gospel. The Gospel of Matthew, while being historical and credible, is also unique in the themes and purpose that Matthew brings out.

Genealogy

You may be tempted only to glance over the genealogy which begins Matthew, but it requires attention. This genealogy is not just a clever way to start out the Gospel, but it is rooted in the Old Testament. Matthew is making a bold claim when he starts out his Gospel with this genealogy, but it links in with the Old Testament genealogies which point to the long-expected Messiah.

All the way back in the Garden of Eden, God makes a promise to the parents of all humanity: Adam and Eve. In Genesis 3:15, God promises that a person, born of a woman, would crush the head of the serpent. From that point on, most of the genealogies which are given are tracing down the line of this promised child. In fact, each one of these genealogies starts with the phrase "The record of the generations of . . ." This is also how Matthew starts his Gospel.

Genesis 5:1–32 narrows down the line from Adam to Noah and his three sons. This genealogy particularly follows the line of Adam's third son, Seth. The firstborn of Adam and Eve is Cain, who killed the second-born, Abel. Genesis 11:10–32 likewise traces the line from Shem, Noah's firstborn, to Terah the father of Abraham. Abraham has no son, and so the next genealogy is in question. But God provides Abraham and Sarah a son in their old age, Isaac. Genesis 25:19 begins with the same formula of "*the records of* the generations of Isaac." But it doesn't list out the descendants of Isaac at this point because Rebekah his wife is barren. But the Lord answered Isaac's prayer on behalf of his wife, and she conceived and bore Esau and Jacob. Even though Esau is the firstborn, the line of the genealogy follows Jacob, who has twelve sons (30). The question then becomes from which of Jacob's descendants will the promised child come. Genesis 49:10, a debated passage certainly, seems to be the first indication that the line will trace through Judah, and this is further verified in Micah 5:2.

In addition, the short book of Ruth shows that God was working in the world to bring about this promised child. This small book is set in the time of the Judges, a period of inconceivable wickedness on the part of Israel. Israel is compared with Sodom and Gomorrah and shown to be as wicked as they were. However, even with all of the wickedness of Israel God was working to preserve the line of the promised child, bringing about the marriage of the Judahite Boaz and the Moabitess Ruth, who then conceived and bore Obed, the grandfather of king David. Ruth 4:18 begins with the statement, "These are the generations of Perez," Perez being a son of Judah.

God also promises king David, from the line of Judah, that there will be a king to sit on David's throne forever (2 Sam. 7). So, this promised child will not only crush the head of the serpent, but he will also be a king on David's throne.

The reason for all of this Old Testament history is to show that Matthew picks up right where the Old Testament left off. Matthew is intentional and deliberate to start out his Gospel with "The record of the genealogy of Jesus." These first words of the Gospel speak volumes, showing that Jesus is the promised child who has been anticipated since Adam and Eve.

Not only should we pay attention to this genealogy, but we should also look at the details of the people in the genealogy. Ruth the Moabitess has already been mentioned. Moabites were pagans who unsuccessfully tried to destroy Israel (Num. 22–25). They also worshipped the false god Chemosh. And Jeremiah, in chapter 48 of his book, prophesies that Moab will be judged because of their wickedness. However, Jeremiah 48:47 says that God will restore Moab in days to come. Ruth is living in a wicked nation surrounded by wicked people. Yet, God brings her out from there, not only to become a follower of the true God, but even to be in the line of the Messiah.

The line starts with Abraham and includes such people as Bathsheba as well as the kings of Judah. This genealogy specifically is tracing the line of Joseph, Jesus' adoptive father. Luke will give one more genealogy which traces the line of Jesus through Mary, and Luke's genealogy will go back all the way to Adam, not only to Abraham. However, Matthew starts his genealogy with Abraham because of his emphasis that Jesus is the Messiah and the king who will sit on David's throne. This leads to another important theme in Matthew, the kingdom of heaven.

The Kingdom of Heaven

King and kingdom are important themes in Matthew. "King" is mentioned eight times, "kingdom" is mentioned fifteen times, and the "kingdom of heaven" and the "kingdom of God" are mentioned thirty-two times and four times respectively. The genealogy establishes Matthew's point that Jesus is the Messiah and the king who is to reign on David's throne. He continues this idea throughout the rest of his Gospel. But the question arises, "What exactly is the kingdom?"

The first words of John the Baptist in Matthew's Gospel are "Repent, for the kingdom of heaven is at hand" (3:2). The first preaching that Jesus did was inaugurated with the words "Repent, for the kingdom of heaven is at hand" (4:17). No explanation is given in either of these contexts expounding on what either John the Baptist or Jesus meant by "the kingdom of heaven." In the same manner as with the genealogy, Matthew is pulling on the Old Testament for explanation. He expects that his readers will be familiar with the concept of the kingdom from the Old Testament. It is not possible fully to understand Matthew without grasping the foundational ideas he is using from the Old Testament.

In simple terms, the kingdom of God is the manifestation of God's rule. But it can be seen in multiple ways. God is sovereign over everything and so His rule extends over the universe. However, God's rule is also working against the powers of rebellion and darkness. There is also an important idea of the culmination of God's kingdom when Christ returns to sit on the throne of David. The kingdom of God, also called the kingdom of heaven by Matthew, is both simple and complex.

Second Chronicles 13:8 links the kingdom of God with the kingdom of Judah. Jeroboam has just started a civil war between the ten northern tribes of Israel and the two southern tribes of Judah, led by Rehoboam, the son of Solomon. Abijah the prophet warns Jeroboam that he is warring against the kingdom of God, since God gave the rule of Israel forever to David and his descendant who will sit on David's throne forever.

Psalm 45:6 says that God's kingdom is forever and is defined by justice. Psalm 103:19 says that God's kingdom rules over everything. Psalm 145:11–13 says that God's holy ones shall speak of the glory of His kingdom forever. But perhaps the greatest insight into the kingdom of God comes from Isaiah. Isaiah 9:1–7 speaks of the coming Messiah. Verse 6 says the government will rest on the shoulders of this Messiah, and there will be no end to His government, ruling from the throne of David. It is this expectation that Israel had even at the time of Jesus' birth.

When Matthew speaks of both John the Baptist and Jesus preaching that the kingdom of heaven is at hand, it is not just the sovereignty of God over all the universe that they are speaking about. It was a kingdom which was described as imminent, soon to be revealed. The response of the people should have been one of repentance. But instead, it was one of rejection of the Messiah as we will see in the sermons of Jesus. Even Jesus' most famous sermon, the Sermon on the Mount, begins with "Blessed are the poor in spirit, for theirs is the kingdom of heaven" (5:3). The kingdom of heaven also belongs to those who are persecuted for righteousness (5:10). The kingdom of heaven will also be filled with people from all over the world (8:11).

Jesus tells his disciples in Matthew 10:7 to continue what both Jesus and John the Baptist began their ministries with, "Repent for the kingdom of heaven is at hand." However, the response of the people to the coming kingdom of heaven is one of violence, hatred, and rejection (11:12). A remarkable shift occurs in the description of the kingdom of heaven from this point on in Matthew. The kingdom of heaven is compared to a farmer, a mustard seed, leaven, hidden treasure, a costly pearl, and many other things. Matthew shows a shift in how Jesus speaks about the kingdom of heaven between Matthew 12 and 13. This will be examined in the sermons of Jesus.

Jesus and the Mosaic Law

Before we examine all the sermons of Jesus in Matthew, we need to better understand Jesus' relationship to the Mosaic Law. And this is established in Jesus' first sermon, Matthew 5–7. Jesus came on the scene preaching "Repent for the kingdom of heaven is at hand." The question that the Pharisees asked is, "What do we need to repent from?" Additionally, the Pharisees questioned what authority Jesus had to demand that they repent. Matthew 9:11 says that the Pharisees questioned Jesus' disciples as to why Jesus was socializing with tax collectors and sinners. In Matthew 12:2, the Pharisees accused Jesus of breaking the Sabbath. In Matthew 19:3 and 22:15 the Pharisees try to trap Jesus by what He said. Jesus exposes the Pharisees as hypocritical, arrogant, legalistic, and unloving (23). Jesus condemns them for not following the law. In Matthew 23:23, He says, "Woe to you, scribes and Pharisees, hypocrites! For you tithe mint and dill and cummin, and have neglected the weightier provisions of the law: justice and mercy and faithfulness." The Pharisees prided themselves on keeping the minutest portions of the law, but Jesus says that they missed the point entirely. Jesus, as the promised Messiah and king, expounds on this idea in His first sermon.

Matthew 5:20 says, "unless your righteousness surpasses *that* of the scribes and Pharisees, you will not enter the kingdom of heaven." Imagine those who were listening to this sermon. They had spent their entire lives looking to the Pharisees to expound on the Mosaic law and exemplify for them what it meant to follow the Mosaic law. The Pharisees strove to keep all the commandments of the Mosaic law, even tithing a tenth of any herbs that they might grow. The Pharisees disdained anyone who had any outward signs of sin in their lives—murders, adulterers, liars, and the like. Jesus turned the pride of the Pharisees on its head.

By stating "You have heard [others say] . . . but I say to you" (5:21–22, 27–28, 31–32, 33–34, 38–39, 43–44), Jesus not only points to the intention of the law, but also places Himself as the authority. The Pharisees, having had their arrogance and manipulative system exposed, react to Jesus as a threat and seek to kill Him.

But Jesus is not throwing the Mosaic law away. Jesus was born under the Mosaic law and even says in Matthew 5:17, "Do not think that I came to abolish the Law or the Prophets; I did not come to abolish but to fulfill." Jesus' fulfillment of the law is not in the likeness of the Pharisees who were only concerned with keeping a series of checkmarks while harboring in themselves wickedness, pride, greed, and malice. Jesus' fulfilling of the law is shown in His keeping of the intention of the law.

No person has ever kept the Law of God except Jesus. The Pharisees prided themselves on not being murderers, but Jesus said that they broke the law "do not murder" by just being angry with someone else. They broke the law against adultery by lusting; they broke the law against lying by simply not letting their yes be yes and their no be no. The intention of these laws is to reveal what is in the heart, not just to keep an outward statute. It is not as though the Pharisees and Jesus are on the same level, debating the correct interpretation of the law. Jesus is saying that He is the authority, even over the Law itself.

The Sermons of Jesus

While there are a few different ways to see the structure of Matthew's Gospel, the sermons of Jesus play an important part in the development of the Gospel. Five sermons are at the heart of the Gospel's message: Matthew 5–7, 10, 13, 18, and 24–25. The two most famous are the Sermon on the Mount (5–7) and the Olivet Discourse (24–25).

Matthew 10 is directed to Jesus' disciples. This is before the leadership of Israel completely rejects Jesus as the Messiah. Jesus sends out the Twelve after giving them authority and power to heal and even cast out demons. In fact, it is here in Matthew 10:2 that the disciples are first called "the twelve apostles." The word "apostle" is from the Greek meaning someone who is sent out. So the disciples, who have been at Jesus' side learning His ways and seeing His miracles, are now the ones being sent out themselves to do the same things. But Jesus takes time to commission His apostles. He instructs them where to go (only to the people of Israel at this time). Their message is to be the same one He and John the Baptist have preached: "Repent, for the kingdom of heaven is at hand" (10:7). They are to perform miracles as a demonstration of their authority and the power of their message. They are to judge who is truly receiving their message and who is not. Those who do not receive the message will be cursed (10:14–15). Jesus encourages the apostles that they will be helped by the Holy Spirit, and also they will be persecuted. A culmination statement of this message is Matthew 10:28, "Do not fear those who kill the body but are unable to kill the soul; but rather fear Him who is able to destroy both soul and body in hell." Jesus emphasizes the sovereign control of God to preserve and empower His gospel. Those who accept the gospel will be rewarded. Those who reject it will be cursed forever.

This is exemplified in Jesus' next sermon: Matthew 13. Matthew 13 is best understood in light of Matthew 12. From the beginning of Matthew's Gospel the refrain has been "Repent, for the kingdom of heaven is at hand." Jesus has performed signs that are indicative of His power and authority as the Messiah. Everything in Jesus' ministry, from His prophesied birth, to His authority in teaching, to His healing of all kinds of sicknesses, and even to His power over demons, has demonstrated that He is the promised Messiah. The question is how will Israel respond. In Matthew 12, the Pharisees respond to Jesus' healing a man on the Sabbath by plotting to kill Him (12:14). Jesus performs another miracle by healing a demon-possessed man. The crowds ask the key question, "This man cannot be the Son of David, can he?" (12:23). The Pharisees respond to this by accusing Jesus of casting out demons by the power of Beelzebul, the ruler of the demons. They attribute Jesus' power and ability to demonic control. Jesus not only points out the insanity of this argument (12:25–27), but He also puts forth an ultimatum, saying that if He is casting out demons by the power of God, then the kingdom of God has come upon them (12:28). In other words, it is time to make their decision about who Jesus is. The Pharisees, as leaders of the people, have committed the blasphemy against the Spirit of God, which will not be forgiven them (12:31). This is what is commonly known as the unpardonable sin. It was committed by the Pharisees, who clearly saw Jesus' power and authority and attributed it to Satan's power. From this point on, Jesus declares that they will not receive any more signs except the sign of Jonah, who was three days and three nights in the deep (12:39–40). In the same way, Jesus will be three days buried and then rise again.

It is after this important encounter with the leaders of Israel that Jesus gives another sermon, Matthew 13. Jesus changes his preaching. It began as straightforward and clear. Now Jesus changes to speaking in parables. Jesus' disciples come to Him and ask why the sudden change (13:10). Jesus responds, "Therefore I speak to them in parables; because while seeing they do not see, and while hearing they do not hear, nor do they understand." Seven parables are given in Matthew 13 which describe the kingdom of heaven. These are the parable of the sower, the tares among the wheat, the mustard seed, the leaven, the hidden treasure, the costly pearl, and the dragnet. Jesus has now turned His face toward Jerusalem, toward His coming death. And it is right after Matthew 13 that John the Baptist is beheaded (14:1–12).

Matthew 18 is the next sermon given by Jesus. This sermon presents a long view. No longer is the kingdom of heaven viewed as being right at hand. Jesus teaches His disciples that they must become like children in order to enter the kingdom of heaven. Jesus' love and care for His people is seen in his parable of the man who goes searching for his one lost sheep (Matt. 18:12–14). This sermon at times even resembles the New Testament epistles with statements like, "If your brother sins, go and show him his fault in private; if he listens to you, you have won your brother" (18:15). Jesus speaks about the authority given to His disciples. He speaks about the church and forgiveness. In this sermon, Jesus takes time to prepare His followers for when He will no longer be with them.

Matthew 24–25 is the last sermon of Jesus in Matthew's Gospel. Matthew 5–7 establishes Jesus' authority; Matthew 10 establishes Jesus' apostles; Matthew 13 responds to Jesus' rejection by the leadership of Israel; Matthew 18 instructs Jesus' followers for after He is gone; and Matthew 24–25 gives the signs for Jesus' return. This sermon is called the Olivet Discourse because it takes place on the Mount of Olives right outside Jerusalem. Jesus' disciples come to Him and ask what will be the sign of Jesus' coming. The answer they receive is probably not what they were expecting. At this moment, they are sitting outside the capital city of Israel. Jesus has just made the triumphal entry into Jerusalem and the crowds met Him shouting Hosanna, which means "save us" (21:9). Jesus has just cleansed the temple (21:12–17). Jesus has responded to the Sadducees and Pharisees such that "no one was able to answer Him a word, nor did anyone dare from that day on to ask Him another question" (22:46). Matthew dedicates all of chapter 23 to Jesus' condemnation of the Pharisees. It is at this point that the disciples come to Jesus to ask what will be the sign of His coming.

The content of this sermon is debated even today. Jesus points to key signs which will precede His return, though at the time, the disciples were not yet aware that Jesus would be betrayed, crucified, resurrected, and ascended into heaven. Jesus explains to His disciples that before His second coming, many people will claim to be Christ. They will mislead many. In addition, there will be wars and famines and earthquakes, though Jesus encourages His followers that they should not be frightened at these things since they must take place before Christ comes back. Christians will even be persecuted and killed for Christ's name. Jesus also declares that the gospel will be preached in all the world before He returns (24:14). Jesus links His prophecy with what Daniel has already said in the Old Testament about an "abomination of desolation" which will be in the temple. After this "abomination of desolation" there will be great tribulation which has not occurred since the beginning of the world (24:21). It is after these things that Jesus will return preceded by the "sign of the Son of Man" in the sky (24:30). This description given by Jesus is meant to spur on His followers to be ready for His coming. The parable of the ten virgins and the parable of the talents (Matt. 25:1–30) emphasize that all who follow Jesus must be ready for His coming and also be good stewards of the time remaining. The great judgment will take place after Jesus returns. This is the culmination of the kingdom of heaven (25:34) in which the wicked will "go away into eternal punishment, but the righteous into eternal life" (25:46).

Study Questions:

1. Why is the genealogy of Jesus so important?
2. Why is Matthew the first book of the New Testament?
3. What is the shift that occurs between Matthew 12 and 13?
4. How would you define the kingdom of heaven?
5. In what way does Jesus establish His authority in the Sermon on the Mount?
6. How would you explain Matthew 5:17 and Jesus' relationship with the Mosaic law?

2

MARK

THE EVIDENCE THAT Mark wrote the Gospel by his name is strong. Just as with Matthew, Mark makes no claim as to authorship, but the early church clearly attests to Mark's authorship of the Gospel. This includes Papias, Irenaeus, Clement of Alexandria, Origen, and Jerome.[1] Additionally, the early church points to the relationship of Peter and Mark in the writing of this Gospel. Mark relied heavily on Peter to produce this work. Donald Guthrie quotes Papias words concerning the authorship of this Gospel:

> Mark indeed, since he was the interpreter of Peter, wrote accurately, but not in order, the things either said or done by the Lord as much as he remembered. For he neither heard the Lord nor followed him, but afterwards, as I have said, [heard and followed] Peter, who fitted his discourses to the needs [of his hearers] but not as if making a narrative of the Lord's sayings; consequently, Mark, writing some things just as he remembered, erred in nothing; for he was careful of one thing—not to omit anything of the things he had heard or to falsify anything in them.[2]

This Mark is mentioned several times in the New Testament (Acts 12:12, 25; 15:37, 39; Col. 4:10; 2 Tim. 4:11; Philem. 24; 1 Pet. 5:13). He was the cousin of Barnabas and was, for a time, rejected by Paul because he left the ministry when things got difficult.[3] However, he was later reconciled to Paul (Col. 4:10), and he was a companion of Peter, as seen in First Peter 5:13.

1 Donald Guthrie, *New Testament Introduction*, 4th edition (Downers Grove, IL: IVP Academic, 1990), 81.

2 Guthrie, 83.

3 Guthrie, 82.

Several scholars have argued for various dates for the composition of Mark. It is probably best to view the date of Mark around the time of Peter's death, with a composition between AD 65 and 68.[4]

Just as with Matthew, it can be difficult to pin down Mark's intended audience. However, the audience of Mark seems to be quite different than that of Matthew. Several details in the text point to this. For example, in Mark 14:12, Mark explains to his audience that on the first day of the feast of Unleavened Bread, the Passover lamb is sacrificed. Mark 15:42 furthermore explains to the audience that there is a day of preparation before the Sabbath. Mark 7:3–4 also explains some of the customs of the Jews in relation to washing hands before eating.

Mark even uses several Roman terms, such as "scourged" (15:15). He compares the coinage of the Jews to the equivalent Roman coin (12:42). Moreover, Mark uses the Roman method of telling time by the watches of the night (6:48). These textual clues point to Mark's intended audience being Gentiles. In addition, it appears that the purpose of Mark was evangelistic. This will be discussed in the section on the gospel in Mark.

Structure

The structure of Mark appears to be split into two major sections: Jesus' ministry in Galilee and Jesus' ministry in Jerusalem. This is bookended with a prologue and an epilogue.

I. The Prologue (1:1–13)
II. The Galilean Ministry (1:14–9:50)
III. The Jerusalem Ministry (10:1–15:41)
IV. The Epilogue: The Resurrection of Jesus (15:42–16:8)

Mark's storytelling is in rapid succession. One of the key words of Mark is "immediately," used twelve times in the Gospel. Mark is quick to point out the key facts and keep the pace moving. This characteristic of Mark stands in contrast to both Matthew and Luke, who take more time giving additional information and description. Mark is focused on the gospel, communicating the necessary details about Jesus to show that He is the Savior of the world.

4 For further discussion on the date of Mark, see Donald Guthrie, *New Testament Introduction*, 84–89. Guthrie gives examples of several scholars who even date Mark in the AD 50s. He also summarizes the early church claims that Mark was written around the time of the execution of Peter.

Purpose

As mentioned above, the purpose of Mark seems to be evangelistic, pointing to the necessary elements of the gospel. Jesus' divinity is on display, and Mark wants his reader to decide to follow Jesus.

Mark Purpose Statement: Believe in Jesus as the Son of God and Savior of the world, and follow after Him.

Themes

One might pull several themes from Mark, and many of these themes overlap with the other Gospels, especially Matthew and Luke. Therefore, some of the themes of Mark will be left for the chapters on Matthew and Luke. However, Mark has a unique focus. Mark is not simply a shorter version of the other Gospels. Mark emphasizes the miracles and power of Jesus which demonstrates that He is the Son of God. Even the description of Jesus' power over demonic forces shows this. Mark gives a quick-fire succession of miracles in chapters 1–9 which point to the gospel and the good news of Jesus. In fact, Mark titles his own writing as "The gospel of Jesus Christ, the Son of God" (1:1). The demonstration of Christ's power forces the reader to confront the Jesus who brings the good news into the world. This is exemplified in Jesus' disciples.

Jesus' Overcoming of Satan's Power

In the Gospels, there is much description of demonic forces. Jesus, along with healing physical infirmities, also casts out demons. In fact, oftentimes, demons are seen as causing some of the physical problems that plagued the people at the time. Satan is also mentioned several times in the Gospels: Three times in Matthew, five times in Mark, five times in Luke, and once in John. Having heard the stories of Jesus' ministry in the Gospels, we do not usually view this demonic activity as being out of place. However, there is a high prevalence of demonic activity in the Gospels as compared with other Biblical books. The Old Testament only has fourteen instances of the title *Satan*, which is simply a Hebrew word meaning "Accuser." Thirteen of the fourteen uses of this word in the Old Testament are with the definite article—"The Accuser." Only once in First Chronicles 21:1 and then in the New Testament is "Satan" used specifically as a name rather than as the title "The Accuser." Also, of the fourteen instances of the word Satan in the

Old Testament, eleven of them are in Job. Ezekiel 28:12–19 also seems to be speaking about Satan's fall, though the title is not used. The term "devil" does not occur in the Old Testament, but it occurs 33 times in the New Testament, fifteen of them in the Gospels.

Indeed, there are a few instances of demonic activity in the Old Testament. King Saul is tormented by an evil spirit in First Samuel (16:14–16; 16:23; 18:10; and 19:9). There are several occurrences of spiritists and mediums in the Old Testament, including the command against mediums and spiritists in Israel (Lev. 19:31). But the first use of the term "demon" occurs in the New Testament. Of the 82 uses of the word "demon" in the New Testament, 66 are in the Gospels.

Matthew 4:1–11, Mark 1:13, and Luke 4:1–13 each recount the story of the temptation of Jesus by Satan. Each account is followed by the beginning of Jesus' public ministry. The question is, why is there is so much demonic and Satanic activity when we move into the New Testament?

It appears that the people at the time were familiar with demonic activity. This also was not just a first-century mistaken understanding of mental illness. The demons that Jesus cast out spoke (Mark 5:12), knew who Jesus truly was in contrast to the people around Jesus (Luke 4:41), and even gave one man the ability to break chains (8:29). The story of the demon-possessed man in the region of the Gerasenes shows that the legion of demons in the man were cast out and subsequently went into a herd of pigs, who then drowned themselves in the Sea of Galilee (Mark 5:1–20).

The Gospels do not explain why there was so much demonic activity at the time of Jesus. Was this also prevalent in the centuries preceding Jesus' birth? In addition, casting out demons was not only accomplished by Jesus. The disciples cast out demons (Matt. 10:8). Mark 9:38 even recounts that others, not just the twelve disciples, were casting out demons. One of the most dire warnings is in Matthew 7:21–23 wherein Jesus says that some will come to Him saying that they cast out demons in His name, and He will tell them that He never knew them.

Jesus' ministry begins with His overcoming the temptation of Satan, and throughout His entire ministry, He is shown to be casting out demons. It appears from these accounts that the people were familiar with demonic activity, though what this looked like in the centuries preceding Jesus is unclear. Satan is depicted as having a great influence in the world. Satan claims to own the kingdoms of the world in Matthew 4:8–10. "Satan," coming from the Hebrew "accuser," and "devil," coming from the Greek word for "slanderer," both point to the primary function of Satan. Jesus even says that the Pharisees' father is the devil in John 8:44 because Satan is the father of lies, just as the Pharisees were slandering Jesus.

A key verse to understand Jesus' interaction with demons and Satan is Mark 3:26: "If Satan has risen up against himself and is divided, he cannot stand, but he is finished!" This is after the Pharisees slanderously say that Jesus is casting out demons by the power of the demons. Jesus clearly points out that only if He is acting on behalf of God can He demonstrate this power over Satan. Jesus' casting out of demons is a sign that He is sent from God. So the Pharisees, as well as all of Israel, have a choice to make: to accept His signs and believe on Him, or to slander Him and reject His authority. Each story of a demon being cast out is a call to believe on Jesus who has the power over all this world.

The Miracles of Jesus

In addition to Jesus' power over Satan and the demons, Mark is quick to show Jesus as a healer and a miracle worker. Mark records nineteen miracles by Jesus, with seventeen in the first half of the Gospel, which is Jesus' Galilean ministry. Mark's account portrays Jesus as gaining fame quickly because of His miracles. The first miracle was the casting out of a demon on the Sabbath in the Capernaum synagogue (1:21–28). The people responded immediately with awe, and soon Jesus was inundated by all in the region who were sick (1:32). In fact, Mark says that the entire city of Capernaum was at the door of the house where Jesus was.

Jesus' fame spread like wildfire, and in a time period of rudimentary healthcare, it is easy to see why. Jesus provided hope to the people, the likes of which had never been seen before. Jesus had all power to heal anyone who came to Him. Mark records the following miracles:

1. Casting out a demon (1:23–28)
2. Healing Peter's sick mother-in-law (1:29–34)
3. Healing a leper (1:40–42)
4. Healing a paralyzed man (2:1–12)
5. Healing a man whose hand was withered (3:1–6)
6. Calming a storm on this Sea of Galilee (4:35–41)
7. Casting out the legion of demons (5:1–14)
8. Raising Jairus' daughter from the dead (5:21–24, 35–43)

9. Healing the woman with the hemorrhage (Mark 5:25–34)
10. Feeding the five thousand (6:30–44)
11. Walking on the Sea of Galilee (6:45–52)
12. Healing many at Gennesaret (6:53–56)
13. Casting out a demon from the Syrophoenician woman's daughter (7:24–30)
14. Healing a man who was deaf and mute (7:31–37)
15. Feeding the four thousand (8:1–9)
16. Healing a blind man (8:22–26)
17. Casting out a demon (9:14–29)
18. Healing blind Bartimaeus (10:46–52)
19. The withered fig tree (11:13–14, 20–22)

These are in addition to statements that Jesus was healing many from town to town (e.g. 1:34). Even as early as Mark 1:45, the Gospel records that Jesus was not even able to go into a city because of His popularity but had to stay in the countryside. People would come to Him from all over the region. Mark 3:9–10 records that Jesus had to have a boat standing by which He could get into because the crowds were pressing in around Him. Everyone who was afflicted was trying to even just touch Him.

Mark contrasts this mad rush for healing with Jesus' statements about concealing His identity. For example, in Mark 1:32–34, the Gospel recounts that Jesus was not allowing the demons which He was casting out to speak, because they knew who He was. After cleansing the leprous man, Jesus warned him not to say anything about Jesus or to tell anyone who Jesus was (1:44). Even in Mark 8:30, Jesus warns His disciples not to tell anyone that He is the Christ, right after Peter's confession that Jesus is the Christ. These statements dominate the first half of the Gospel. Once Jesus sets His face toward Jerusalem (Mark 10:1), these statements cease. The Triumphal Entry of Mark 11 shows that Jesus presents Himself as the Messiah. Even before this point, when the rich young ruler comes to Him in Mark 10:18, Jesus asks him why he called Jesus "good," since no one is good except God alone.

Jesus has compassion on the sick and the demon-possessed. He demonstrates His compassion throughout his Galilean ministry by healing everyone who comes to Him. These healings are a sign of Jesus' power, but also of His messiahship. Matthew 8:17 says that Jesus' healing ministry fulfilled the prophecy of Isaiah 53:4, which speaks of the Messiah carrying away our disease.

We must remember that Jesus Himself was born under the Mosaic Law. The requirements concerning cleansing in the Mosaic Law were still in effect. For example, Leviticus 13 lays out the laws for skin diseases. If someone had a skin disease, such as leprosy, they were pronounced unclean by the priest. Leprosy was a particularly awful disease since there was no hope of a cure. It was also easily transmitted, so those who had the disease were isolated and cut off from the community. A leper colony was the only hope of meaningful human interaction. In the first chapter of Mark, the fame of Jesus spreads to such an extent that a leper hears of Jesus, goes to Him, falls on his knees, and begs to be healed (1:40). What is fascinating about this story is that the leper says "If you are willing, You can make me clean." The last recorded story of a leper being healed was Naman, who lived almost a millennium before this leper came to Jesus.

Jesus, moved with compassion, stretches out His hand and touches the leper and heals him. We should see Jesus' compassion and love for the man in this story. But what we should also see is that Jesus touched the man for his healing. A vast portion of the Mosaic Law is centered around what to do when you come into contact with the unclean. Leviticus 5:2 is an example. If someone was to touch something dead or even a living unclean animal such as a mouse or a pig, they had to cleanse themselves, whether through a ritual bath or through a sacrifice. In other words, the clean is defiled by the unclean. According to the Mosaic Law the unclean is not made clean by contact. It is the other way around. Jesus turns this on its head. Jesus is not defiled by the leper; instead, Jesus' touch makes clean what was formerly unclean. Jesus did not have to undergo a ritual cleansing after He touched the leper. Instead, the leper was now healed, and he was to go to the priest to be pronounced clean—something that, before he met Jesus, he never expected would ever happen to him.

Jesus' miracles were signs, pointing to His messiahship. Each one demonstrated in a unique way that Jesus was the long-expected Messiah. And this Messiah was not like any man who had come before, unable to escape sin and uncleanness in the world. These miracles were a visible manifestation of the good news that Jesus brought into the world.

The Gospel

Mark starts out with the phrase, "The beginning of the gospel of Jesus Christ, the Son of God." The word *gospel* in the Greek means "good news." Since Mark begins his Gospel this way, the question is, *what is the gospel?*

What is contained within this good news? Much of the good news is seen in the opening verse. Jesus, a man who is born of Mary, is also the Christ, the Messiah. And Jesus is also the Son of God. These introductory elements point us to how Mark is defining this good news.

The word *gospel* comes up again in Mark 1:14–15. The gospel is what Jesus began preaching, "The time is fulfilled, and the kingdom of God is at hand; repent and believe in the gospel." These demonstrate additional elements that we must take into consideration. We have examined the idea of the kingdom of God in the chapter on Matthew. Those elements need to be brought to bear on what the gospel is. God's rule and reign coming through King Jesus is imminent. This has been prophesied about and when Jesus came, the time was fulfilled.

Repentance and belief is also shown to be part of the gospel. This is not just repentance and faith in general. The repentance spoken of here in Mark is in stark contrast to the hard-hearted Pharisees and others who clutched onto their arrogance and self-reliance rather than trusting in Jesus. Repentance and faith are two sides of the same coin, always going hand in hand. True repentance is not accomplished without faith in the Savior. Mark's description of the gospel is centered on Jesus, who paves the way for this good news.

Mark 8:35 also points to the price: "For whoever wishes to save his life will lose it, but whoever loses his life for My sake and the gospel's will save it." Just preceding this statement, Jesus says, "If anyone wishes to come after Me, he must deny himself, and take up his cross and follow Me." This gospel of repentance and faith is not accomplished in tandem with your old nature but rather by overcoming it. The one who seeks to preserve his life, to keep what he has and is, will, in the end, lose what he has been seeking. The one who repents, turns to faith in Christ, will gain true life. Mark is not ambiguous on the nature of the gospel.

Mark also points to the reward of the gospel. Mark 10:29–30 states,

> Truly I say to you, there is no one who has left house or brothers or sisters or mother or father or children or farms, for My sake and for the gospel's sake, but that he will receive a hundred times as much now in the present age, houses and brothers and sisters and mothers and children and farms, along with persecutions; and in the age to come, eternal life.

Jesus is saying that one family is traded for another. The point of the passage is not that believing the gospel will produce wealth for you. Rather, believing the gospel places you into the church family. You lose one family, even being ostracized for the sake of the gospel; and you replace that family with your new family.

Mark continues to clarify the gospel in Mark 13:10. Jesus is speaking of the second coming and the end of the age. Mark 13 parallels much of Matthew 24–25. Before Jesus will return, "The gospel must first be preached to all the nations." This was a radical shift in thought for the Jewish nation at the time. They believed they had the truth, the revelation of the Mosaic law. And they insulated themselves from the other nations. Jesus declares the opposite, that the truth of the gospel will be proclaimed in every nation before He comes back. Jesus also points to the persecution that will arise before He returns. Half of the occurrences of "gospel" in Mark are in contexts of persecution. Mark leaves no doubt that the followers of the world's system will persecute Jesus' disciples. This echoes Matthew 10:34 in which Jesus says that He has not come to bring peace but a sword. The gospel results in persecution of Jesus' followers by those who refuse to repent.

The last instance of the term *gospel* in Mark is set within a beautiful story of the woman who poured the costly perfume on Jesus' feet before He was to be killed. She recognized that Jesus was going to His death and she anointed his body beforehand for the burial (14:8). Jesus says, "Truly I say to you, wherever the gospel is preached in the whole world, what this woman has done will also be spoken of in memory of her" (14:9). This woman's faith is contrasted with Judas immediately afterward, as Judas left to seek a way to betray Jesus.

Mark speaks of the gospel simply. But the good news also has many aspects to it. It is the untwisting of a perverse world, the kingdom of God come to destroy the kingdom of darkness and deliver those who turn in repentance and faith to Jesus the Savior. The gospel brings division and persecution. The gospel brings about a new family. The gospel gives hope of eternal life. And the gospel is centered around Jesus' work, His power being demonstrated through miracles and signs and ultimately through His resurrection.

The Disciples

The disciples of Jesus are key figures in all the Gospels. They are listed out in Matthew 10, Mark 3, and Luke 6. The twelve are:

1. Simon, whom Jesus renamed Peter
2. Andrew, the brother of Simon Peter

3. James, the son of Zebedee
4. John, the brother of James
5. Philip
6. Bartholomew, who is also called Nathanael
7. Matthew, the tax collector
8. Thomas, who is also called Didymus meaning "the twin"
9. James, the son of Alphaeus
10. Thaddaeus, who is also called Judas
11. Simon the Zealot
12. Judas Iscariot

Of these twelve, Peter, James, and John play the leading roles. They are the ones to see Jesus' transfiguration (Mark 9:1–8). When Jesus raises Jairus' daughter from the dead, it is only Peter, James, and John that Jesus permits by His side (5:37). Jesus also takes Peter, James, and John with Him further into the Garden of Gethsemane (14:32–33).

Peter makes the confession that Jesus is the Messiah in Mark 8:29. Peter is often the first to speak up, sometimes getting himself in trouble. Mark 14 recounts Peter's denial of Christ. James and John have the nickname "sons of thunder," and they request of Jesus that they sit on His right hand and on His left hand in His glory (10:35–40). This audacious request shows their initial self-centered thinking. Luke also recounts a story of Jesus and His disciples being rejected by a Samaritan village. Luke 9:54–55 states, "When His disciples James and John saw *this*, they said, 'Lord, do You want us to command fire to come down from heaven and consume them?' But He turned and rebuked them."

Jesus called Bartholomew (also known as Nathanael) "an Israelite indeed, in whom there is no deceit" (John 1:47). Matthew worked for the Romans as a tax collector, hated by his own people because of extortion. Simon the Zealot was part of a violent radical religious sect. Thomas is known as the doubter. And the most infamous disciple is certainly Judas the betrayer.

The faults of these disciples are seen throughout the Gospels, even in their abandonment of Jesus in the Garden of Gethsemane. However, what is fascinating to see is their humility after the events described. For example, in the three lists of the disciples in Matthew, Mark, and Luke, only Matthew calls himself "the tax collector." Mark and Luke do not give him that title in their lists. Additionally, John doesn't even call himself by his own name in his Gospel. These are men who were transformed by their Savior. Certainly, we can see the transformation of Peter, from a hothead to someone who gave his life for the gospel. It was only through the transforming power of the gospel that these men were emboldened to stand for the truth against the most powerful people at the time, even giving their lives for the gospel.

Study Questions:

1. Why does Mark give so many examples of Jesus' miracles in the first half of his Gospel?
2. Why does Jesus try to keep his identity as the Messiah a secret for the first half of Mark?
3. Why do the Gospels have so many stories about demon-possessed people in contrast to so few examples in the rest of the Bible?
4. Why do you think that Mark moves his story along so quickly? Why is Mark so much shorter than the other Gospels?
5. What would you say are the necessary elements of the gospel?

3

Luke

THE EARLY CHURCH clearly attests to Luke being the author of both the Gospel of Luke as well as Acts.[1] These two served as a two-volume compilation to present both the history of Jesus' ministry as well as a history of the early church. Luke was both a doctor and a traveling companion of Paul, as evidenced by the first-person plural ("we") narratives in Acts (Acts 16:10–17; 20:5–15; 21:1–18; and 27:1–28:16). In Colossians 4:14, Paul calls Luke the "beloved physician." The Gospel of Luke also demonstrates a sophisticated use of the Greek language, which would be expected from an educated person.

Since the two volumes of Luke are linked, this helps to date both books. Acts 28:30–31 ends this two-volume set with Paul being held prisoner in Rome, awaiting trial. It would be odd for Luke not to mention the outcome of the trial if it had happened prior to Luke's writing of these volumes. Therefore, the best dating of the Luke and Acts would be before the end of Paul's first imprisonment, around AD 58–60.[2]

The audience of Luke is listed as a single person whose name is Theophilus. In Greek, this name means "lover of God." Nothing else is mentioned about Theophilus, which leads many to believe that this name stands for anyone who loves God. The name is Greek, which may indicate that Luke intends his audience to be Gentile Christians. In addition, this lengthy account is characteristically different from Mark, which is short and decidedly evangelistic. Luke plans to detail and describe the life of

1 For a summary of the evidence of Lukan authorship from the early church, see Andreas Köstenberger, Scott Kellum, and Charles Quarles, *The Cradle, the Cross, and the Crown: An Introduction to the New Testament* (Nashville: B&H Publishing, 2009): 258–261.

2 For further description of the different debates surrounding the dating of Luke and Acts, see *The Cradle, the Cross, and the Crown*, 261–264.

Christ, not necessarily exhaustively but in an orderly way which is in line with what has been handed down to Luke.

Luke makes clear that he is not an eyewitness. He is writing this first volume based on his research and engagement with those who were eyewitnesses. Luke is part of the second generation being raised up in the teaching of Christ. Luke emphasizes that he has investigated everything carefully from the beginning of Jesus' life until the present time at which he is writing. Luke, more than any of the other Gospels, makes an ardent claim of historicity. Each Gospel has a purpose and a theological argument. But that does not negate the historical claims that they make. It is the purpose and theological argument which makes each Gospel unique, which is why there are four Gospels and not simply one lengthy historical retelling of the life of Jesus.

Structure

The structure of Luke is quite similar to a letter. There is an opening salutation directed to Theophilus. Luke presents his goal for the Gospel in the first few verses. There seems to be a prologue in which Luke spends considerable time speaking about the anticipation of the births of both John the Baptist and Jesus. Luke is also the only one who spends time telling a story about Jesus' childhood when he was twelve years old, found in the temple by his parents. Once this prologue finishes, Luke begins the story of Jesus' ministry, breaking it down into Jesus' preparation for ministry, His ministry in Galilee, His ministry on the way to Jerusalem, and His ministry while in Jerusalem. The Gospel ends with the events of Jesus' death, resurrection, and ascension, which will lead directly into volume two, the book of Acts. In this way, the structure can be seen as follows:

I. Salutation (1:1–4)

II. Prologue (1:5–2:52)

III. Jesus' Preparation for Ministry (3:1–4:13)

IV. Jesus' Ministry in Galilee (4:14–9:50)

V. Jesus' Ministry on the Way to Jerusalem (9:51–19:27)

VI. Jesus' Ministry in Jerusalem (19:28–21:38)

VII. Jesus' Death, Resurrection, and Ascension (22:1–24:53)

PURPOSE

The purpose of Luke's writing is also spelled out in the introduction. Luke tells Theophilus that he is writing this Gospel "so that you may know the exact truth about the things you have been taught" (1:4). Luke intends to draw up an account of the "things accomplished among us" (1:1). The "us" he is referring to are apparently his fellow Christians. This orderly account is not only comprised in the Gospel of Luke but also in the second volume, Acts. Therefore, the purpose of this Gospel is intertwined with Acts.

> **LUKE PURPOSE STATEMENT:** To compile a detailed account of the outworking of God's sovereign plan to bring about salvation through the Lord Jesus Christ.

This purpose statement for Luke should also be read in light of the purpose of Acts which will be to show God's sovereign plan in establishing the church, the body of believers who share in the salvation of Jesus Christ.

THEMES

Luke emphasizes God's sovereignty throughout his Gospel. Luke sees every bit of the ordering and orchestrating of events which he describes in Luke 1:1–4 as being from the hand of God. The wording that Luke uses to describe his curated stories points to his theological argument that God is in complete control, bringing about redemption through Christ at the right time. Christ as the Son of Man is also an integral part of the sovereign plan of God. Luke's retelling of the birth of Jesus begins his Gospel with this key concept: God the Son has taken on a human nature. This Son of Man concept is central to Luke's argument and also has its foundation in the Old Testament. Additionally, we will look at baptism in Luke. Luke emphasizes the idea of baptism, though it is also seen in the other Gospels. Baptism must be understood from the Old Testament as well. It was not something new that John the Baptist inaugurated. Additionally, Luke places great weight upon the outcasts of society. Luke spends time giving detail and pointing to events which demonstrate Jesus' care and concern for the wretched. Finally, we will look in detail at the timeline of the last week of Jesus, from entering Jerusalem to His resurrection.

God's Sovereignty in Salvation

Both Luke and Acts emphasize the sovereignty of God. An important example of this is Jesus' statement that the Son of Man is going to be betrayed "as it has been determined; but woe to that man by whom He is betrayed!" (Luke 22:22). Luke recognizes again and again that the events which have occurred have been orchestrated by God.

Luke points to the fulfillment of the prophecies in the Old Testament. Jesus says the prophecy of Isaiah 61:1 has been fulfilled at the start of Jesus' public ministry (4:18–21). Jesus also says, "Behold, we are going up to Jerusalem, and all things which are written through the prophets about the Son of Man will be accomplished. For He will be handed over to the Gentiles, and will be mocked and mistreated and spit upon, and after they have scourged Him, they will kill Him; and the third day He will rise again" (18:31–33). Jesus knew exactly what was to happen to Him because it was the purpose and plan of God, which was not to be thwarted. Luke 22:37 is another example of Jesus pointing to Old Testament prophecy and showing its fulfillment in Him.

Additionally, eighteen times in Luke, the Greek work *dei* is found, which is usually translated as "it is necessary." Jesus says it is necessary that He preach the gospel in many cities besides Capernaum (4:43). Jesus says it was necessary that the Son of Man suffer many things and be rejected (9:22). Jesus even says that it was necessary that he stay at Zaccheus' house (19:5). According to Luke and the other Gospels, these events were all part of God's plan and orchestrated by His sovereignty.

It is also important to note that Jesus points to Old Testament prophecy which is not fulfilled during Jesus' life on earth. Luke 21:22–24 says that it is necessary that Jerusalem be "trampled underfoot by the Gentiles until the times of the Gentiles are fulfilled." These times of the Gentiles precedes Jesus' second coming (21:25–28). Just as it was certain that Jesus would die and be resurrected at the time He was, so it is also certain that He will return. And the signs which precede His return are also certain.

This leads to the question of culpability. Matthew 27:24 is a famous picture of Pilate, the Roman governor of Judea, washing his hands at the trial of Jesus and saying, "I am innocent of this Man's blood." Pilate consents to the riotous crowd and releases Barabbas, a known murderer, instead of Jesus. Jesus is crucified, but Pilate tries to demonstrate that he is not guilty of Jesus' death.

The Pharisees and Judas would be another example. God sovereignly orchestrated that Jesus would be rejected, mocked, and killed. This was to bring about salvation. Is God holding Judas culpable for the betrayal of Jesus even though God sovereignly brought it about? This is a question that has been debated for many centuries. Luke presents us with two clear facts:

1) God sovereignly brought about the death of Jesus for the purpose of the salvation of His children, and
2) Those who rejected Jesus, betrayed Him, and murdered Him are guilty (Luke 22:22).

The malice that filled the hearts of the Pharisees and Judas came from their own natures. Their rejection of Jesus brought about by their own pride and wickedness culminated in their attempt to kill Jesus. God made use of that wickedness to bring about His own purposes. Just as Joseph says to his brothers in Genesis 50:20, "As for you, you meant evil against me, *but* God meant it for good in order to bring about this present result." God works sovereignly in the lives of humans to bring about His purposes, even working through the wicked decisions of humans.

The Son of Man

Twenty-five times Luke uses the title "Son of Man." All the Gospels use this title frequently. In Luke, Jesus first refers to Himself as the Son of Man in Luke 5:24, saying that the Son of Man has the authority to forgive sins. Luke 6:5 says that the Son of Man is Lord of the Sabbath. This places the Son of Man as the authority over the Mosaic Law, which had the Sabbath as its sign. Luke 6:22 says that you are blessed if you are persecuted for the sake of the Son of Man, because your reward is great in heaven. Luke 7:34 says the Son of Man is a friend of sinners. The Son of Man must suffer according to the purposes of God (9:22). The Son of Man will determine who enters into glory (9:26; 12:8; 21:36). The Son of Man has no true home on the earth (9:58). The Son of Man is coming again at an hour when He is least expected (12:40; 17:24–30; 21:27). A theme verse is Luke 19:10, "The Son of Man has come to seek and to save that which was lost." The Son of Man is now seated at the right hand of God in majesty (22:69).

This title is based on the prophecies of Daniel. When Jesus applies this title to Himself, He is saying something more specific than just that he is human. Daniel 7:13–14 says:

> I kept looking in the night visions, /And behold, with the clouds of heaven /One like a Son of Man was coming, /And He came up to the Ancient of Days /And was presented before Him. /And to Him was given dominion, /Glory, and a kingdom, /That all the peoples, nations and *men of every* language /Might serve Him. /His dominion is an everlasting dominion /Which will not pass away; /And His kingdom is one /Which will not be destroyed.

It is from this prophecy and description that the Pharisees and Jews at the time of Jesus understood what He meant by the Son of Man. When Jesus first refers to Himself as the Son of Man, Luke does not record anyone asking what He meant or why He was referring to Himself with this title. The words were enough to link back to Daniel 7:13–14. The description that Daniel gives also links the Son of Man with the Messiah, the one who was to be the Ruler on David's throne forever. The kingdom which is given to the Son of Man in Daniel 7 is the Davidic kingdom based on Second Samuel 7. This will be an everlasting dominion which will fulfill what God promised to David in the Davidic Covenant.

The prophecy in Daniel 7:13–14 has not been fulfilled at this point. Jesus points to this in Mark 14:62 when He says to the Sanhedrin, "You shall see the Son of Man sitting at the right hand of Power, and coming with the clouds of heaven." The high priest believed that this claim by Jesus was enough to condemn Jesus for blasphemy. Jesus, as the Son of Man prophesied about by Daniel, is sitting at the right hand of the Father and will come again.

After the Gospels account, Stephen is the next to speak of the Son of Man. Stephen is stoned in Acts 7 for being a follower of Jesus. Right before Stephen is stoned to death, Acts 7:55–56 says:

> But being full of the Holy Spirit, he gazed intently into heaven and saw the glory of God, and Jesus standing at the right hand of God; and he said, "Behold, I see the heavens opened up and the Son of Man standing at the right hand of God."

Revelation also makes use of this title for Jesus. The apostle John in Revelation 1:13–15 describes the Son of Man:

> *I saw* one like the Son of Man, clothed in a robe reaching to the feet, and girded across His chest with a golden sash. His head and His hair were white like white wool, like snow; and His eyes were like a flame of fire. His feet were like burnished bronze, when it has been made to glow in the furnace, and His voice *was* like the sound of many waters.

This description of the Son of Man is seen in other places in the Old Testament such as Ezekiel 1. Revelation 14:14 links the Son of Man with the judgment which is coming on the earth in the last days. All of this description brings together a picture of the Son of Man, from Daniel to the Gospels to Acts 7 to Revelation. Jesus, the lowly baby laid in a manger, is also the Son of Man who is at the right hand of the Father now. He is coming again in power and glory to judge. His kingdom will be an everlasting kingdom, and all the earth will be subject to Him.

Baptism

Luke spends considerable time speaking about John the Baptist. Luke records the story of how John received his name. Luke spends ten verses speaking about the birth of John the Baptist, more than any other Gospel. Luke describes the fact that John lived in the desert until the day of his public appearance to Israel (1:80). With all of the description given about John, Luke does not explain why John was baptizing. Luke 3:3 simply says, "And he came into all the district around the Jordan, preaching a baptism of repentance for the forgiveness of sins." The fascinating thing that happens is that huge crowds were coming down to John from Jerusalem to be baptized by him.

The question that arises is, what did they understand about baptism? No one in the passage seems confused as to why John is dunking people under water as he preaches about repentance. They recognize what is going on and the people flock to John from Jerusalem to hear his message, many of them being baptized by John as well. The people were even wondering if John was actually the Messiah. John clarifies with this statement: "As for me, I baptize you with water; but One is coming who is mightier than I, and I am not fit to untie the thong of His sandals; He will baptize you with the Holy Spirit and fire" (3:16).

Because baptism is a common occurrence in the church today, we often forget how it would have been viewed at the time of John. Where did baptism come from? Why was it linked with John's ministry? How is it that Jesus baptized with the Holy Spirit and fire? And another important question is, why was Jesus baptized?

Baptism has a long biblical history. John did not invent baptism; he was pulling on a long-standing practice with deep significance. A key passage to understand baptism is First Corinthians 10:2. In this text Paul says that Israel was baptized into Moses in the Red Sea. This baptism was a deliverance for Israel from the Egyptians, but it was not true salvation, since Paul goes on to say, "Nevertheless, with most of them God was not well-pleased; for they were laid low in the wilderness" (1 Cor. 10:5).

The question is what it means that they were baptized into Moses. Moses was the leader who brought them down into the waters of the Red Sea and then led them up to the other side. They were relying on Moses for deliverance, and Moses was acting according to God's commands. This historical account of the crossing of the Red Sea is used by Paul to illustrate a picture of going down into the water of judgment and coming out on the other side as a sign of deliverance. Israel went down into the Red Sea, following after Moses. Because they were led by Moses they were delivered on the other side. In contrast, the Egyptians went down into the Red Sea and were buried in the waters of judgment.

The water signifies the judgment from which someone must be delivered. The picture is that if one is not delivered from the judgment, then that person would stay under the water permanently. Being raised on the other side of the water is a demonstration that the water of judgment cannot hold you. The people at the time of John the Baptist went out to him, listening to his teaching. Those who repented of their sin were baptized to show that by their repentance, they escape the judgment to come. The water baptism signified this, and the people who were baptized by John understood this sign. John's baptism was not something new that no one had ever seen before.

The question remains as to why Jesus would need to be baptized. Luke records Jesus' baptism, "Now when all the people were baptized, Jesus was also baptized, and while He was praying, heaven was opened, and the Holy Spirit descended upon Him in bodily form like a dove, and a voice came out of heaven, 'You are My beloved Son, in You I am well-pleased'" (3:21–22). It was possible for someone to go through the physical sign of baptism by John and not actually have repented of their sin. Several, certainly, underwent baptism but did not change their ways. John told the soldiers whom he baptized that they should not steal money by force or accuse anyone falsely (3:14). John told the tax collectors whom he baptized that they should not collect more than what they had been ordered to collect (3:13). Certainly, there were soldiers who were baptized by John who continued to steal money by force and tax collectors who extorted the people. The baptism, after all, was just a physical sign of a hoped-for reality: That the person had truly repented and would change. Jesus undergoes baptism to demonstrate that He is pure, not subject to the judgment of God. Jesus did not need to repent of anything, nor do any of the Gospels say that He repented before He was baptized. Jesus' baptism was not subsequent to His repentance, but rather Jesus' baptism was a sign that He had no need to repent. Matthew 3:15 records that Jesus told John that His baptism was to "fulfill all righteousness." This was a sign of Jesus' innocence and pure character, which immediately preceded Jesus' temptation by the devil, in which Jesus absolutely proves this fact.

In addition to the baptism itself, the Father and the Holy Spirit testify to the same thing. The Father speaks from heaven, declaring that in Jesus He is well-pleased. No fault can be found in Jesus. The Holy Spirit descends and rests on Jesus to show His perfect fitness for the ministry He is about to begin. The testimony of the Father and the Holy Spirit reveal the truth which the baptism signified.

In addition, it is also important to understand what John means by Jesus' baptizing by the Holy Spirit and by fire. John's baptism was only a symbol. John did not have the authority to condemn. John was only an instrument to pave the way for the coming of the true Judge. Fire is the picture of the ultimate and final judgment. In contrast, being baptized with the Holy Spirit is the seal of one's salvation. Israel was baptized into Moses, which provided a temporary salvation from their enemies and from judgment. John's baptism was only a symbol, but baptism by the Holy Spirit is part and parcel of true salvation from the judgment of God. Jesus is the one who baptizes with the Holy Spirit for salvation.

The Outcasts of Society and the Gentiles

Luke pays special attention to the those at the time who were considered lower in society. He mentions the poor eleven times, starting with Jesus' quotation of Isaiah 61:1 on the Sabbath. In Luke 4:14, Jesus begins His public ministry after being tempted by the devil. Luke records that Jesus went into the synagogue in Nazareth on the Sabbath. He stood up to read a section of the Old Testament to the congregation, and this is what He chose in Luke 14:18–19:

> The Spirit of the Lord is upon me /Because He anointed Me /To preach the gospel to the poor. /He has sent Me to proclaim release to the captives, /And recovery of sight to the blind, /To set free those who are oppressed, /To proclaim the favorable year of the Lord. (Isa. 61:1; also quoted in Matt. 11:5 and Luke 7:22)

Jesus informs the congregation that this scripture has been fulfilled that very day because Jesus had begun His ministry. Jesus focused His gospel toward those in need. Truly all are in need of the gospel, but Jesus reminds His listeners in Luke 5:31–32, "*It* is not those who are well who need a physician, but those who are sick. I have not come to call righteous but sinners to repentance." This was directed against the Pharisees, who believed that they were not in need of a doctor. Even though they were in dire need of salvation, their arrogance blinded their eyes.

In contrast, Luke portrays the poor, the needy, and the destitute as recognizing that they need deliverance. Jesus even begins His beatitudes with "blessed are you *who are* poor, for yours is the kingdom of God" (Luke 6:20). In Luke 14:7–15, Jesus admonished guests who had been invited to a dinner. They had been picking seats of honor for themselves, and Jesus reproved them to instead sit in the lowly positions, "For everyone who exalts himself will be humbled, and he who humbles himself will be exalted" (14:11). He also warned them not to invite their rich friends and relatives to their feasts, but rather to invite the poor, the crippled, the lame, and the blind who have no way to repay them; then they will have true reward with God.

Luke is the only Gospel to tell the parable of Lazarus. There is even some debate as to whether this is actually a parable or a true story. But in this story, Jesus contrasts a rich man, who remains unnamed, with a poor beggar, Lazarus. Both of them die and Lazarus goes to heaven while the rich man is tormented in hell. In the story it is revealed that the rich man spent his life pursuing the pleasures of the world and invested nothing in eternal things. Lazarus placed his faith in God to deliver him (16:19–31).

Jesus does not say that all rich people will go to hell. The question is whether the rich person values their wealth over eternal life. The rich young ruler comes to Jesus to ask about salvation, but instead rejects Jesus' teaching because He told him to sell all that he had and give it to the poor (18:22). Jesus says, "How hard it is for those who are wealthy to enter the kingdom of God! For it is easier for a camel to go through the eye of a needle than for a rich man to enter the kingdom of God" (18:24–25). This stood in contrast to the culture at that time. The Jews of the first century believed that if someone was rich, it was because they were righteous, and God was blessing them financially as a reward. Jesus reminded them that wealth is not a sign of spiritual maturity. In the examples of wealth in the Gospels, more often than not the rich valued their physical wealth more than eternal life.

In addition to the poor and destitute, Luke also emphasizes the role of the Gentiles in the ministry of Jesus. Jesus is said to be "A light of revelation to the Gentiles" (Luke 2:32 which is taken from Isaiah 9:2; 42:6; 49:6; 51:4; and 60:1–3). Jesus contrasts the response of the Gentiles to the gospel with that of the Jews at that time. He even points to the Old Testament when He says:

> There were many widows in Israel in the days of Elijah, when the sky was shut up for three years and six months, when a great famine came over all the land; and yet Elijah was sent to none of them, but only to Zarephath, *in the land* of Sidon, to a woman who was a widow. And there were many lepers in Israel in the time of Elisha the prophet; and none of them was cleansed, but only Naaman the Syrian (Luke 4:25–27).

Individual Gentiles who came to Jesus are shown to accept the gospel. This is seen with the Roman Centurion in Luke 7:1–10. It is seen even with the Samaritans in the parable of the Good Samaritan (10:25–37). Luke also records that of the ten lepers that Jesus healed at one time, it was only the Samaritan leper who came back to give Him thanks (17:12–19).

A third group that Luke highlights are the women who were involved in the ministry of Jesus. Of all of the Gospels, Luke pays special attention to these women. In the culture at the time of Jesus, the impact and influence of women was oftentimes overlooked. However, Luke emphasizes the faith and devotion of both Mary, the mother of Jesus, and Elizabeth, the mother of John the Baptist (e.g., 1:5–6, 28, 42). It is a woman who shows the greatest repentance (7:37–50). Mary Magdalene plays an important role in Luke (8:2; 24:10). On the way to the cross, Jesus addresses the women in the crowd who were weeping for Him (23:27–31). Luke points out the women who had accompanied Jesus and His disciples from Galilee (23:49). It was the woman who prepared the burial ointment for Jesus (23:55–56). And it was women who were first to the tomb to see the evidence of the resurrection (24:22).

Timeline of Jesus' Crucifixion, Death, and Resurrection

Each of the Gospels records the last week of Jesus from a different perspective, all of them historically accurate. Compiling the Gospels' accounts will give good insight into the time from Jesus' entering Jerusalem to His resurrection. However, there is debate as to how the events of Jesus' last week fall on the days of the week.

John 12:1 says that Jesus came to Bethany, just outside of Jerusalem, six days before the Passover, which began on a Friday evening. Counting back six days from Passover, Friday evening, would bring us to Saturday evening when Jesus arrived in Bethany. There is some debate about whether this was

Saturday evening or Sunday. Jesus has dinner in the house of a man called Simon the Leper. This is where the woman, whom John identifies as Mary the brother of Lazarus, anointed Jesus' feet with the vial of costly perfume (John 12:1–8). Interestingly, Matthew and Mark both reflect on this story, putting it out of order chronologically in order to place it closer in their story to the telling of Jesus' death (Matt. 26:6–13; Mark 14:3–9).

The next day, Sunday, Jesus makes His triumphal entry into Jerusalem (Matt. 21:1–11; Mark 11:1–10; Luke 19:29–44; John 12:12–19). The people took palm branches and laid them before Jesus. The palm is a symbol of kingship. For example, King Solomon had palm branches, lions, and cherubim engraved together in the temple (1 Kings 7:36). Revelation 7:9 depicts a scene in heaven where a multitude is holding palm branches before the Lamb. Isaiah 9:14 uses the bulrush to symbolize the lowly in Israel and the palm to symbolize the leadership in Israel. In the triumphal entry, the crowds are demonstrating that they want Jesus to be their king, even calling Him the King of Israel (John 12:13). After the triumphal entry, Jesus goes to the temple on the same day and then returns to Bethany to spend the night (Mark 11:11).

The next day, Monday, Jesus, on the way back to Jerusalem, curses the fig tree as a sign of Israel not bearing fruit as they should (Matt. 21:18–19; Mark 11:12–14). Jesus, upon entering Jerusalem again, cleanses the temple (Matt. 21:12–13; Mark 11:15–18; Luke 19:45–48). After this, Jesus returns to Bethany to spend the night (Mark 11:19).

The next day, Tuesday, Jesus gives the lesson of the fig tree to His disciples. Jesus had cursed the fig tree the day before, and His disciples realized as they were passing by it the next day that it had withered from the roots up (11:20–26).

Jesus spends considerable time in the temple on Tuesday as well. He is confronted by the Jewish leaders who ask, "By what authority are You doing these things, or who gave You this authority to do these things?" (11:28). Jesus responds to them with a question about John the Baptist, which they cannot answer. Jesus gives the parable of the vine-growers (12:1–12), which spoke against the Jewish leaders. Mark 12:12 says that the leaders were trying to seize Jesus, but they did not yet seize Him because they were afraid of the people. They then proceed to try to trap Jesus in His words by asking about paying taxes to Caesar (12:13–17), by asking about resurrection (12:18–27), and by asking Jesus what is the greatest commandment (12:28–34). Jesus answers all questions wisely and then asks His own question, which stumps the Jewish leaders (12:35–37). Jesus condemns the Jewish leaders and pronounces His seven woes on the scribes and Pharisees (Matt. 23). It is after this point that Jesus leaves the temple, goes to the Mount of Olives, and gives the Olivet Discourse (24–25). After Jesus finished saying these things, the plot to kill Jesus builds (26:1–5) and Judas goes to the chief priests and asks what they will pay him to betray Jesus (26:14–16).

Wednesday seems to be a silent day, in which there is no record in the Gospels of what Jesus and His disciples did that day. This is where some of the debate exists as to which days these events fall on. Some attempt to explain this by moving all the prior days up by one day. In other words, the triumphal entry would have been on Monday, not Sunday, and so on and so forth. However, it is probably best just to see that the Gospel writers did not record anything for this day.

On Thursday, Jesus begins to make preparations for the Passover. Now this timeframe can be tricky to understand. The key to understanding the timeline of Passover is to see how Passover and the Feast of Unleavened Bread were to work together. In Leviticus 23:5–8, we see that Passover was on the evening preceding the beginning of the Feast of Unleavened Bread. Passover was one day, from sunset to sunset. The Feast of Unleavened Bread was to begin the following day and last for seven days. There is also some debate as to whether individual families observed Passover in their own homes on one day, while the next day Passover was observed for the entire nation, centered at the temple. In this way, Jesus has the disciples start making preparations for the Passover on Thursday morning, planning on observing Passover on Thursday at sunset. Thursday at sunset would start the Passover, which would end at sunset on Friday. The chief priests planned to hold their celebration in tandem with the first day of the Feast of Unleavened Bread, starting Friday at sunset. Therefore, the Jewish leaders plan to kill Jesus on Friday before sunset so that they can still observe the celebration.[3]

Therefore, on Thursday, Jesus and the disciples make preparations for the Passover. They hold Passover in the Upper Room (Matt. 26:20–29; Mark 14:17–25; Luke 22:14–38; John 13:1–17:26). It is here that Jesus washes His disciples' feet. Judas also leaves from the Upper Room to confirm his betrayal of Jesus to the Jewish leaders, leading them to Jesus just hours after eating with Him in the Upper Room.

---

3 For a detailed examination of these days, see Joachim Jeremias, *The Eucharistic Words of Jesus* (London: SCM Press, 1966).

Once Jesus finishes the Passover meal in the Upper Room and after praying the High Priestly Prayer of John 17, He and the disciples move to Gethsemane. Matthew 26:36–56, Mark 14:32–52, Luke 22:40–53, and John 18:2–12 all recount Jesus' time in Gethsemane, when Jesus prays in anguish to His Father, that the cup of wrath might pass from Him. Jesus submits to His Father's will and is arrested by the Jewish leaders after they are led to Jesus by Judas, who later hangs himself on Friday (Matt. 27:3–10).

On Friday before the rooster crows, Jesus is taken to trial by the Jewish leaders. They take Jesus from the Garden of Gethsemane to Annas' house (John 18:13–23). Annas was the father-in-law of Caiaphas. Caiaphas held the position of high priest, but it was really Annas who was the de facto leader. The position of high priest at this time was not as much a religious position as it was a political position. Jesus is then moved to Caiaphas' house (Matt. 26:57–75; Mark 14:53–72; Luke 22:54–65; John 18:24–27). Caiaphas and the rest of the Jewish leaders condemn Jesus for blasphemy after they are unable to procure witnesses against Jesus who agree. Jesus says that He is the Son of Man and the Son of God, which Caiaphas takes as blasphemy. Luke 22:66–71 records that Caiaphas moved Jesus from his house to stand before the whole Sanhedrin, the Jewish ruling body. It is from here that Jesus is taken to Pilate (Matt. 27:2, 11–14; Mark 15:2–5; Luke 23:1–5; John 18:28–38). Pilate, the Roman governor, finds no fault in Jesus and sends him to Herod, son of Herod the Great, who tried to have Jesus killed as a baby. Herod the Great was long dead, but his kingdom, given to him by Rome, had been divided into multiple sections, one of which was ruled over by Pilate. Another portion of Herod the Great's kingdom was ruled over by his son, also called Herod. Luke 23:6–12 records that Herod found no fault in Jesus and sent Him back to Pilate.

Jesus stands before Pilate a second time (Matt. 27:15–26; Mark 15:6–15; Luke 23:13–25; John 18:39–19:16). Jesus is scourged and beaten on Pilate's orders. Pilate thinks that this will suffice for the Jewish leaders, and they will lose their taste for blood. However, the Jewish leaders double down their efforts. Pilate tries to free Jesus through the annual custom that he has to release a prisoner each year on Passover. But the Jewish leaders call for Barabbas to be released instead of Jesus. Pilate washes his hands and commands the soldiers to take Jesus out to be crucified. Matthew 27:27–56, Mark 15:16–45, Luke 23:26–52, and John 19:17–30 recount the various details of Jesus being first condemned and then moved to Golgotha, where he was to be crucified. At Jesus' crucifixion, the soldiers divide up

His garments by casting lots (Matt. 27:35). They place a sign over Him which reads "This is Jesus the King of the Jews" (27:37). Two robbers are crucified with Him as well, one of whom turns in repentance.

Matthew records that from the sixth hour (noon) until the ninth hour (3 p.m.), there was darkness over all the land (27:45). Jesus died around the ninth hour, roughly three hours before the Jewish leaders planned to start their own Passover. The Gospels record seven sayings of Jesus from the cross. And after Jesus died, there was an earthquake, the curtain of the temple was torn in two from top to bottom, and many in their tombs were brought back to life (Matt. 27:51–53). The centurion testified that Jesus was the Son of God. And at evening, Joseph of Arimathea requested the body of Jesus from Pilate for burial (27:57–61). The Jewish leaders placed guards at the tomb of Jesus the next day (Saturday).

Saturday, Jesus is in the tomb (Matt. 27:60–66; Luke 23:56). Jesus is resurrected from the dead Sunday morning, having been a portion of three days in the grave (Friday evening, Saturday, and Sunday morning). Matthew 28:1–8, Mark 16:1–8, Luke 24:1–43, and John 20:1–23 recount the details of the resurrection, how two women were first to the tomb to see the evidence of the resurrection. Two angels tell Mary Magdalene and Mary the mother of James that Jesus was resurrected. They report this to the disciples, and Peter and John run to the tomb to see. The body is gone, and they report back to the disciples. John 20:11–18 reports that Jesus first appeared to Mary Magdalene. Jesus then appears to two other women in Matthew 28:9–10. This same day, Jesus appeared to two of His disciples on the road to Emmaus (Luke 24:13–35). Jesus appeared to Peter after this in Luke 24:34. Ten of the disciples are the next to see Jesus (24:36–43; John 20:19–23).

It is after this that Jesus appears to many others in the time which followed, leading up to Jesus' ascension to heaven to the right hand of the Father. Jesus appears to the eleven disciples, including doubting Thomas, in John 20:24–31. Jesus appears to seven of the disciples while they are fishing in Galilee in John 21:1–23. Jesus appears to the eleven disciples in Galilee in Matthew 28:16–20. First Corinthians 15:7 records that Jesus also appeared to James. And Jesus appeared to the eleven disciples in Jerusalem in Luke 24:44–49 (also seen in Acts 1:3–8).

Study Questions:

1. How is Luke different from Matthew and Mark? Why was it necessary that Luke's Gospel also be written?
2. How does Luke emphasize God's sovereignty in the events of his Gospel?
3. In what Old Testament passage does the phrase "Son of Man" find its foundational meaning? What does this title mean?
4. Why did Jesus need to be baptized? What does First Corinthians 10:2 mean by saying Israel was baptized into Moses?
5. What was the final accusation by which the Jewish leaders condemned Jesus to death?

4

Acts

THE AUTHOR OF ACTS IS certainly Luke. Though not an apostle nor an eyewitness of Jesus, Luke is a historian. He has compiled the facts, speaking with those who were eyewitnesses of Jesus' life. Luke is also a dedicated Christian and companion of Paul. It is important to notice the change in Acts to the "we" statements. Paul begins his second missionary journey in Acts 15:36. Initially, Luke speaks of Paul in the third person (e.g., "he was traveling through Syria and Cilicia," Acts 15:41). However, Luke switches to first person in Acts 16:10: "When he had seen the vision, immediately we sought to go into Macedonia, concluding that God had called us to preach the gospel to them." Luke, without mentioning his own name, places himself into the narrative, because it was at this point that Luke joins Paul on his second missionary journey. No mention is made of Luke's conversion. Immediately before this, Timothy is introduced. Luke spends time explaining who Timothy is. He was from the area of Lystra and Derbe. His mother was Jewish, but his father was a Greek. Timothy was converted and began to accompany Paul on this missionary journey. This description is in contrast with Luke, who does not mention his own conversion nor how he first met Paul. While Luke does not give much description of himself, we can see where Luke accompanied Paul on his journeys because of this use of first person in the narrative.

Interestingly, Luke's name is only mentioned three times in all of the New Testament, even though he authored two books in the New Testament. In Colossians 4:14, Paul calls Luke "the beloved physician." It is only by this description that we learn that Luke was a physician. We do not know anything more about his practice. This word for physician is only used a handful of times in the New Testament. Mark 5:26 uses the word to speak about the woman who had a hemorrhage for twelve years, and says that this woman "had endured much at the hands of many physicians, and had spent all that she had and was not helped at all, but rather had grown worse." The physicians in this case were unable to heal, which shows why the woman was so desperate for a cure.

It is impossible to know how long Luke spent as a physician. Where had he studied? Was he a practicing physician before meeting Paul? Did he continue as a physician while traveling with Paul? The only insight that we gain is through Paul's calling Luke a physician.

In Second Timothy 4:11, Paul says that Luke is still with him. This is the last of Paul's epistles, a heartfelt and weighty letter that he writes to his disciple Timothy. This letter was written right before Paul is executed on Nero's command. The only one who is with Paul is Luke. It is likely that it was only Luke with Paul at the very end of his earthly life. The book of Acts stops with Paul's first imprisonment, several years before his execution. From the end of Acts to the execution of Paul, Luke stands by his side. Paul rightly calls Luke his fellow worker in Philemon 24. These are the only three instances of Luke's name in all the New Testament.

The date of Acts has already been cursorily discussed in the chapter on Luke. It is best to see Luke and Acts as having been written around the same period, as they are volume one and volume two of Luke's work. The best way to date Acts is by the ending of the book. Luke ends Acts with Paul awaiting his first trial in Rome. This would have been around AD 62. From other records such as Second Timothy, it becomes evident that Paul was released from his first imprisonment in Rome. After the book of Acts, Paul continues to minister and travel, preaching the Word of God. It is subsequent to this that Paul is arrested again, perhaps due to Nero's persecution of the church which begins in AD 64.[1] After Paul writes Second Timothy, he is executed. But no mention of this is made in Acts. Nor is there a mention of the destruction of Jerusalem in AD 70. It is best to see this evidence as pointing to the writing of Acts c. AD 62.

The recipient of Acts, Luke names as Theophilus. This may be the name of an individual or it may stand for anyone who loves God, as the name means "one who loves God." This type of address may also be seen in Second John, when John writes his second epistle to "the chosen lady and her children." The debate, which is further explored in the chapter on Second John, is that John is speaking metaphorically, the chosen lady representing the church and her children representing the members of the church. It is not without precedent

1 Donald Guthrie, *New Testament Introduction*, 4th edition (Downers Grove, IL: IVP Academic, 1990): 360.

that a writer would address an individual as a representative of a larger group. It is probably best to see Theophilus as pointing to those who love God. For more discussion on Theophilus, see the chapter on Luke.

STRUCTURE

The structure of Acts can be broken down into two parts. The book contains a preface (1:1–2) which links this book back with the Gospel of Luke. Luke mentions his first account, and also mentions that he is writing this volume to Theophilus. Luke connects his previous volume with this new volume and spends nine verses (1:3–11) pointing to Jesus' ascension, which he also briefly mentioned in Luke 24:50–53. It is after this point in Acts that Luke turns his attention to the remaining apostles. The rest of the book of Acts is centered around the apostles' work. From Acts 1:12–12:24, Luke emphasizes the work of the apostles in and around Jerusalem, ministering to the Jews. This includes the conversion of Saul, later to be known as the apostle Paul. From Acts 12:25–28:31, Luke changes the focus, directing it to the ministry to the Gentiles. The structure can be broken down accordingly:

- I. Preface (1:1–11)
- II. The Apostles' Witness to the Jews (1:12–9:31)
  - a. Jerusalem (1:12–6:7)
  - b. Beyond Jerusalem (6:8–12:24)
- III. The Apostles' Witness to the Gentiles (12:25–28:31)
  - a. Establishing Paul's Apostleship (12:25–16:5)
  - b. Paul's Expanded Work toward the Gentiles (16:6–19:20)
  - c. Paul's Ministry Moved to Rome (19:21–28:31)

PURPOSE

The purpose of Acts is to report the sovereign work of God in establishing the church. Luke's intention is to relate the events of the early church, but Luke also has a theological purpose in writing. He is not simply a historian who is trying to tell facts. Acts has a theological goal, to show the reader God's sovereign working in the early church. This does not discount the historicity of Acts. Luke does not change any of the historical facts to fit this theological purpose. Rather it is these very facts which should be understood as coming from the hand of God. Luke seeks to show how the gospel spread from Jerusalem all the way to Rome, from eleven apostles and a handful of people in Jerusalem to churches all over the Roman world. This gospel moved from a few fishermen to being spoken before kings. This is all due to the working of God, just as Jesus testified in Matthew 16:18, "I also say to you that you are Peter, and upon this rock I will build My church; and the gates of Hades will not overpower it."

> **Acts Purpose Statement:** To demonstrate the sovereign work of God in establishing the church from Jerusalem to Rome, proclaimed to both Jews and Gentiles.

Themes

It is important to remember that Acts is not simply a history book. Luke records historically accurate facts about the early church, but Acts also contains intentional theological themes and ideas which are seen throughout the book. The most prominent is the work of the Holy Spirit. If the Gospel of Luke focuses on Jesus, then Acts continues the story of the Gospel by focusing on the continued work of the Holy Spirit. We should see the sovereign work of God in building His church just as He promised.

This is done through people. The Holy Spirit uses many people in Acts to bring about the plan of God. Philip goes to Samaria. Apollos from Alexandria preached the Word of God mightily. Lydia is the first convert in Europe. In the book of Acts, no two human figures play as significant a role as Peter and Paul. These two will be examined each in their own sections. Another theme to notice is the obedience of the church. The church follows the lead of the Holy Spirit. Those who only pretend to obey the Holy Spirit are found out. This will be exemplified in the story of Ananias and Sapphira in Acts 5. Throughout Acts people are confronted with the powerful truth of the gospel and their decisions are made clear. From the Ethiopian eunuch accepting the gospel to the rejection of the gospel by Felix in Acts 24. The acceptance or rejection of the gospel by individuals is on display throughout Acts.

The Holy Spirit's Work

The Holy Spirit's work is truly the central focus of Acts. It is the baptism of the Holy Spirit which inaugurates the church (Acts 2:38). The Holy Spirit also demonstrates who is truly a believer. This is seen throughout Acts. We must remember that the early church did not yet know its own character. It is over time that the Holy Spirit exposes the truth about what God has intended the church to be and to do. The gift of tongues is one example of this.

The church began as a group of Jewish believers. As other groups began to accept the gospel, the church grew into a multiethnic and multinational entity. It was the Holy Spirit who demonstrated this. First, the church is born on the day of Pentecost, which was fifty days after the Passover. It is on this day that those who had followed Christ were all gathered together in one place. The Holy Spirit filled them and they began to speak in tongues (Acts 2:1–4). This was not a sign that the people understood. Remember, when John the Baptist started to baptize, the people all understood the sign and symbol of baptism. They did not need John to explain the significance to them. But in this case, the people who were close by did not know what was going on. The gift of tongues, given by the Holy Spirit to those who were following Jesus, was the ability to speak in other languages, previously unknown to the speaker. The example of tongues in Acts 2 was not babbling or random sounds but rather known languages. Acts 2:8 is the question of those who were nearby and heard, "And how is it that we each *hear* them in our own language to which we were born?" This powerful act by the Holy Spirit was a reversal of the dispersion of the rebellious people at the Tower of Babel. The Tower of Babel was a judgment of God against a rebellious people, causing new languages which could not be understood by other groups (Gen. 11:1–9). By the work of the Holy Spirit, the gospel was going out, breaking past language and cultural barriers.

Each time there is a question about who else is part of the church, the Holy Spirit demonstrated who had been saved. Philip went down to Samaria to preach the gospel, and the Samaritans received the Holy Spirit (Acts 8:17). The Gentiles also received the Holy Spirit and spoke in tongues (10:45–46). Even when there was a question about some of the disciples of John the Baptist, the Holy Spirit evidenced that they also had been saved and were now part of the church (19:1–10).

In addition to this, the Holy Spirit guided the mission work done in Acts. Acts 13:2 says, "While they were ministering to the Lord and fasting, the Holy Spirit said, "Set apart for Me Barnabas and Saul for the work to which I have called them." The church immediately responds in obedience and sends Paul and Barnabas away to their work. In Acts 16:7, it is the Holy Spirit who prevents Paul from going to the area of Bithynia, instead sending him and his companions to Macedonia to minister there. This work of the Holy Spirit shows the sovereign work of God and also the fulfillment of the promise of Jesus to send the Spirit who is called the Helper (John 15:26). While many individuals are mentioned in Acts, the book is really about the work of the Holy Spirit in directing, leading, preserving, protecting, and instructing the church.

Peter

The chapter on Mark has already discussed some of Peter's life. Acts continues to add to the description of Peter. He was a quick-tempered man who was making a living as a fisherman in Galilee when Jesus called him. Peter's character is on display in many stories of the Gospels, and the Gospels also portray Peter as a leader among the disciples. He continues to be a leader in Acts. It is Peter who gets up to speak after the outpouring of the Holy Spirit on the day of Pentecost.

Soon after Jesus' betrayal and Judas' suicide, Peter stands up in front of the other disciples and says that they should choose someone to replace Judas (1:15–26). Interestingly, many of the other disciples, named in the Gospel accounts and also listed in Acts 1:13, are never mentioned again in the New Testament. But Peter is seen as the leader and takes the primary role in Acts until the focus shifts to Paul.

It is Peter who heals a lame man, giving the first miracle of healing in Acts. The lame man was sitting at the temple, asking for money (3:1). He does not notice Peter or pay attention to him until Peter stops in front of him and tells him to walk, healing his lameness (3:1–10). Acts does not portray Peter as being weak or fearful. Peter is the one who points out the wickedness of Ananias and Sapphira, who fall dead at his feet (5:1–16). Peter goes to prison for his faith, expecting to be executed (12). It is Peter and John who are sent to verify that the Samarians have accepted the gospel and been included in the church (8:14). Even though Paul is called the Apostle to the Gentiles, it is Peter who receives the vision from God and is sent to the house of Cornelius to demonstrate that the Gentiles are also to be saved and brought into the church.

There is some evidence that Peter had a wife, though no mention is made of their having children. Jesus heals Peter's mother-in-law in Matthew 8:14–17. In addition, Paul alludes to the fact that Peter was married in First Corinthians 9:5, seeming to indicate that Peter took his wife along with him while he traveled preaching the gospel.

While Acts focuses away from Peter after chapter 12, the early church's tradition was that Peter was executed around the time that Paul was also executed.[2] This would have been during Nero's persecution of the church. According to tradition, Peter was crucified, hung upside down on the cross. This was alongside his wife, who was also martyred for her faith in Christ.

Paul

We are able to piece together much of Paul's life after his conversion.[3] We also know some of the details of his life before his conversion. Saul, who later came to be called Paul (Acts 13:9), is not mentioned in any of the Gospels. No mention is made as to whether he was in Jerusalem at the time that Jesus was crucified. The first mention of Saul is Acts 7:58. Those who stoned Stephen, the first Christian martyr, laid their coats at Saul's feet before they went to stone Stephen. This was a sign of the approval that Saul was giving to this martyrdom. Immediately after the stoning of Stephen, Saul becomes a leader of the persecution against Christians. Acts 8:3 says, "Saul *began* ravaging the church, entering house after house, and dragging off men and women, he would put them in prison." Saul eventually leaves Jerusalem, going to Damascus to persecute more Christians. It is on the way to Damascus that he is converted, being blinded by a great light and hearing Jesus ask, "Saul, Saul, why are you persecuting Me?" (9:4).

We also gain more insight into Paul's life before his conversion from other texts. For instance, from the story of Paul's arrest in Philippi, we learn that Paul was a Roman citizen (16:37). He was not born in Rome, but rather in Tarsus (21:39), and Paul was born a Roman citizen (22:28). Paul states in Acts 22:3 that he studied under the Pharisee Gamaliel who also appears in Acts 5:34, giving advice to the Sanhedrin not to kill Peter and the rest of the apostles when they refused to obey the Sanhedrin's command not to preach. Philippians 3:5 says that Paul was of the tribe of Benjamin, a Hebrew of Hebrews. Paul sought salvation through works before his conversion, a story similar to Martin Luther many centuries later. Those who seek salvation by works only succeed in exhausting themselves, trying to find some assurance of salvation. Jesus turns that misguided work in Paul into passion and love for the church. Paul, the one who persecuted the church, is converted and becomes the greatest missionary of the early church.

In Galatians, Paul says that he did not receive the gospel which he preached from any man, but directly from Christ Jesus (1:11–12). Paul says

2 Donald Guthrie, *New Testament Introduction*, 1004.

3 For a helpful summary of the chronology of Paul's life, see Donald Guthrie, *New Testament Introduction*, 1004–1010.

that right after his conversion, he did not go to Jerusalem to be with the apostles; instead, after having his sight restored in Damascus, he went to Arabia and then returned to Damascus. Paul says that after three years he went up to Jerusalem to spend time with Peter (Gal. 1:18), after which he went to Syria and Cilicia, most likely back to Tarsus which is in the region of Cilicia. It is during this time that the church begins to accept his former persecutor into the fold. Barnabas plays a key role in this. Acts 9:27 says that Barnabas took Paul to the apostles, vouching for his conversion and newfound love for the church. Barnabas took Paul from Tarsus to Antioch (11:25–26) and spent one year there strengthening the church in Antioch.

Paul and Barnabas are then sent off on their first missionary journey, which lasted for approximately one year. Acts 13–14 records this journey, which departed from Antioch and went to the island of Cyprus and then sailed from Paphos to Perga in Pamphylia (13:13) and went to Pisidian Antioch. It was at this time that John Mark, the future author of the Gospel of Mark, abandoned Paul and his companions and returned to Jerusalem. Paul did not view this abandonment well, and refused to take Mark on the second missionary journey (15:39). Paul and his companions were not welcomed by the Jews in Pisidian Antioch, and so they left and traveled to Iconium. After Paul preached in the synagogue in Iconium, a plot was formed to stone him and his companions, so they fled to Lystra. It was in Lystra that Paul healed a lame man (14:8–11). However, some of the Jewish leaders followed Paul from Pisidian Antioch and Iconium and stirred up the crowd in Lystra. Paul was stoned by a mob and left for dead (14:19). However, Paul got up and went back into the city, the next day going on to Derbe. Luke reports that there were many converts in Derbe, and Paul and his companions returned from there back to Antioch, from where they had begun their journey. Paul most likely wrote the letter of Galatians after having established churches in this southern Galatian region which included Psidian Antioch, Iconium, Derbe, and Lystra. This would make Galatians the first of Paul's epistles.

Paul's second missionary journey is recorded in Acts 15:36–18:22 and lasted approximately three years. It was Paul's idea to return to those cities he had visited previously. Barnabas wanted to take John Mark, but Paul was unwilling, so Barnabas took Mark and went to Cyprus. Paul took Silas and traveled through Syria and Cilicia (15:41). Paul went back to Lystra and Derbe, finding Timothy there. Timothy then began to accompany Paul on his second missionary journey. Paul moved to the Galatian region and the

Holy Spirit eventually led the group to go to Macedonia. It is at this point that Luke adds himself into the story, apparently joining Paul in Troas before they all went on into Macedonia (16:8–10). Paul moved from Philippi to Thessalonica, Berea, Athens, and Corinth. Paul most likely wrote First Thessalonians in the early part of AD 51.[4] Paul stayed for eighteen months in Corinth and wrote Second Thessalonians from Corinth as well. It was after this stay in Corinth and the penning of these two letters that Paul returned to Jerusalem, ending his second missionary journey.

Paul's began his third missionary journey soon after. This is recorded in Acts 18:23–21:16 and took about five or six years. Paul went through the Galatian region, eventually traveling to Ephesus, where he spent two years. Acts 19:9–10 says that Paul taught in the "school of Tyrannus" for these two years, building up the churches in and around Ephesus. This was one of the most fruitful and encouraging times for Paul. It was in Ephesus that Paul wrote First Corinthians, perhaps around spring of AD 56, based on the chronology of Acts. Paul had actually written a previous letter to the Corinthian church before his letter of First Corinthians. He mentions this letter in First Corinthians 5:9–11. After writing First Corinthians, Paul went to Macedonia. Second Corinthians 12:14 and 13:1–2 seem to indicate that Paul visited Corinth a second time before writing Second Corinthians, which he sent from Macedonia. Paul then, after sending Second Corinthians, went to visit Corinth for a third time. This would have been around the end of AD 56 and the beginning of AD 57. While in Corinth, Paul wrote Romans, having heard of the faith of the Roman church but not having visited Rome yet.

It was at this point that Paul began his journey back to Jerusalem, wishing to be there before Pentecost (Acts 20:16). Paul arrived in Jerusalem and was very quickly arrested on the charge of stirring up dissension and defiling the temple (21:28). Paul spent the next two years (24:27) standing trial before several Roman leaders and avoiding plots against his life (23–26). Paul eventually appealed to Ceasar, since he was a Roman citizen, and was

4 Donald Guthrie explains this date: "The date of this epistle may be fixed with a fair degree of precision since it falls within Paul's period at Corinth, which provides us with one of the most certain contacts with secular chronology in the proconsulate of Gallio. According to an inscription at Delphi, Gallio was proconsul during the twelfth year of Claudius' tribunicial power and after his twenty-sixth proclamation as Emperor. This must have been before August 52." Paul appeared before Gallio in Acts 18:12–18, thereby helping to date Paul's time in Corinth. Paul wrote First Thessalonians shortly after arriving in Corinth. See Donald Guthrie, *New Testament Introduction*, 587–588.

taken by ship to Rome. It was while Paul was imprisoned that he took up his pen and wrote four more letters: Ephesians, Philippians, Colossians, and Philemon. It is in Acts 27 that Luke recounts the story of Paul's shipwreck. We must also remember that Luke himself was a part of this shipwreck on Malta. It took Paul more than three months to travel to Rome (Acts 28:11). Luke ends Acts with the following words: "And he stayed two full years in his own rented quarters and was welcoming all who came to him, preaching the kingdom of God and teaching concerning the Lord Jesus Christ with all openness, unhindered" (28:30–31).

While the book of Acts does not speak to this, we know from history that Paul was released from this imprisonment. His plan, as he told the Romans, was to travel to Spain. It was after Paul had been freed that he wrote First Timothy and Titus. Second Timothy was written after Paul was arrested and sent to Rome a second time. In Second Timothy, Paul writes that he expects to be executed (4:6). At the command of Nero, the apostle Paul was indeed executed, though the exact date is not known.

Peter and Paul seem to have very different personalities, but God used them both mightily. It is interesting how Acts speaks about Peter and Paul in similar terms. Acts 4:8 speaks about Peter as being filled with the Holy Spirit. The same is said of Paul in Acts 13:9. Interestingly, Luke gives narratives of both Peter and Paul healing a lame person, Peter in Acts 3:1–10 and Paul in Acts 14:8–10. In addition to this, both are described as even raising up a dead person. Peter raises up a woman named Tabitha from the dead in Acts 9:36–43. Paul raises up Eutychus from the dead after he falls out the window in Acts 20:9–12. Both Peter and Paul have a run-in with a sorcerer (Acts 8:9–24 and 13:6–12). Both are miraculously released from prison, Peter in Acts 12:1–8 and Paul in Acts 16:22–30. Both men have a vision while praying (10:10 and 22:17). An angel speaks to both on separate occasions (12:7–8 and 27:23–24). Acts also records three sermons by each man. Peter preaches in Acts 2, 3, and 10; Paul preaches in Acts 13, 14, and 17. While these men have very different personalities, Luke points to many similarities of how God worked through them.

One other point to make is that Peter and Paul did not always agree. Just because these two men authored Scripture and were apostles of Jesus does not mean that they were infallible. When they were inspired by the Holy Spirit, they wrote infallible and inerrant passages of the New Testament. But in their lives, they were still sinners, fallible men in need of God's salvation. Galatians 2:11–21 records an instance where Paul confronted Peter about a sinful decision. Paul, in this epistle to the Galatians, recounts that Peter gave in to pressure by Jews who believed that they were better than the Gentiles. Paul says that after these Jews came to Antioch, Peter would not even eat with the Gentiles because of this desire to please these Jews. Paul confronts Peter, who repents. In addition, Paul speaks of himself as being the chief of sinners as discussed earlier. Paul and Peter were not superhuman. They were fallible, ordinary people that God used to do extraordinary things. They would both point to this and give God all the glory for the work that He is doing.

The Obedience of the Church

Luke records a remarkable description of the early church. Acts 2:41 records 3,000 people being saved in one day, and Acts 2:42 says, "They were continually devoting themselves to the apostles' teaching and to fellowship and to the breaking of bread and to prayer." Luke describes the early church as being of one accord. Persecution united the church, especially as we see with Peter's arrest by Herod in Acts 12. He intended to execute Peter, but the Lord delivered him, freeing him from the prison miraculously. The more that the Jewish leaders try to quiet the church, the more that it grows and flourishes.

Acts 2:44–45 says, "And all those who had believed were together and had all things in common; and they *began* selling their property and possessions and were sharing them with all, as anyone might have need." This sets up the story in Acts 5 of Ananias and Sapphira. On the surface, this may seem like a harsh story. This married couple sold a piece of property and with his wife's knowledge gave only a portion of it to the apostles, intending to deceive them as though he had given them the whole amount. Peter confronted Ananias and said that the property was his and the proceeds from the property were his. He could have kept the entire amount if he wished. The apostles were not expecting that everyone sell all that they have and give the proceeds to them. Rather, Ananias and Sapphira's sin was that they sold the property and pretended to give all the proceeds to the apostles. Their deceit was based on pride and a desire for admiration. The apostles did not require them to give any money to the church, but they believed they would be able to get away with this deceit. Peter knows immediately what they have done and confronts Ananias. Immediately, Ananias is struck down by God and dies. Three hours later, his wife comes into the same place, not knowing what happened to her husband. She utters the same lie her husband did, and she also is struck down by God. The sin was not that they didn't give everything to the church. The sin was that they lied to the church. While this seems harsh, it demonstrates the purity of the early church.

Another example of this is found in First Corinthians 11:30. Paul tells the Corinthians that there were several in the Corinthian church who had taken the Lord's Supper unworthily, not examining themselves but eating in a gluttonous or unworthy manner. It was for this reason that several people in the Corinthian church had died. Paul indicates that God had killed them because they did not honor the Lord's Supper as they should have. Many signs and miracles are done by the apostles in Acts, but Luke also points to God purifying the early church. Luke's description is that the church was of one mind, learning from the apostles, accepting the doctrines of Christ, continually devoted to prayer and to the Lord's Supper, and giving generously and sacrificially. Those who tried to deceitfully imitate this were removed from the church, even by God striking them down. This is not always the case, however. As the church grows it is no longer depicted as it was at the beginning. In First Corinthians, Paul mentions that God has struck down those who were taking the Lord's Supper in an unworthy manner. But in the Corinthian church there were many other problems that Paul was addressing. By the time we get to John's letters to the seven churches, there is description of the love of some churches growing cold. There were some heresies which had crept into the church. Even Third John depicts a church leader who needed to be exposed for arrogance. The church was never perfect, but Acts does point to a beautiful time at the inauguration of the church wherein the church was dedicated wholeheartedly to the gospel and to its divine call to be a light in the world.

Study Questions:

1. How is the description of the Holy Spirit's work in Acts a fulfillment of Jesus' promises to His disciples?

2. In what ways is the early church a model for the church today? Should we follow everything that the early church did or are there any things which were unique to the church at that time?

3. Why do you think that Peter and Paul are described in similar ways, accomplishing similar miracles and having similar visions?

4. Is tongues a spiritual gift for today or was it just a sign given to the early church by God? What about the gift of healing, such as Peter and Paul had?

5. How is the story of Paul's life an example of the sovereign work of God? How is it that God would allow someone who is dedicated to furthering the gospel to be executed (see Phil. 1:21)?

PART TWO

Johannine Literature

5

John

THE GOSPEL OF JOHN gives several hints as to the authorship. Just as with the other three Gospels, there is no explicit claim of authorship in the text. The titles "According to Matthew," "According to Mark," or "According to Luke" were added after the original Gospels were written. They are early signs of authorship, and the early church can provide a great deal of evidence for authorship, but there is no direct attestation of authorship in any of the Gospels. However, the Gospel of John does have some unique hints to authorship. This includes the fact that the disciple John is never mentioned by name in the Gospel. The apostle John is instead called "the disciple whom Jesus loved." John 21:24 is the closest identification of the author, "This is the disciple who is testifying these things and wrote these things, and we know that his testimony is true." The author also uses the first person in several instances such as John 1:14, "We saw His glory." This places the author as an eyewitness of Jesus' ministry. These allusions point to the apostle John as the author of the Gospel.[1]

The dating of John is helped by understanding the purpose. As will be seen in the section on the purpose of John, the apostle set out to write a Gospel different than the other three, while recognizing the full authority and veracity of the other three. But John would have written his Gospel after the other three had been composed.

In addition to placing John after the other three Gospels chronologically, there are other factors that help to narrow down the date, though there is nothing definitive. There is evidence of the Gospel being used early in the second century.[2] Since the apostle John was the author, this would also limit

1 For further insight on debates on the authorship of John, see Donald Guthrie, *New Testament Introduction*, 4th edition (Downers Grove, IL: IVP Academic, 1990): 252–283.

2 Donald Guthrie, *New Testament Introduction*, 297.

the time frame of the composition to earlier than AD 100. Irenaeus claims that John lived up until the reign of Trajan which began in AD 98.[3] The best understanding of the time of the Gospel's composition would be in the AD 90's, but it is difficult to pin down an exact year with any confidence.

John's intended audience seems to be virtually unlimited. Based on the purpose statement, which is evangelistic, John is writing with a very broad audience in mind. While there are many Jewish elements throughout the Gospel, it is not specifically written to a Jewish audience; that is more the characteristic of Matthew.

Why would John feel the need to add an additional Gospel which emphasizes Jesus' divinity (see the section on purpose)? Was he trying to combat an errant view of Jesus' nature? Several have claimed that John was trying to combat Gnosticism, a heretical teaching stemming from Greek philosophy.[4] The Gnostics believed that the material world is evil, and therefore they denied that Jesus could have taken on a true human nature or body. Gnosticism didn't really reach its peak until well into the second century AD, though John could have been engaging with early elements of Gnosticism. All in all, it is best to see John's work directed to those who need to understand that Jesus was both fully human and fully divine.

Structure

John, like many of the other Gospels, has an important prologue. This prologue is one of the pinnacle passages concerning Jesus' nature, along with Colossians 1 and Hebrews 1. John 1:1–18 summarizes the Word of God, who was made flesh. From John 1:19–12:50, the signs are given which testify to this. Chapters 13–20 speak of the Messiah and the church. The first half of the book shows the proofs of both Jesus' divinity and humanity. The second half of the book switches to speak more of Jesus' message to the church. This would include Jesus' High Priestly Prayer and an extended message during the Last Supper. There have been a few different arguments for the structure of the Gospel, but it is important to recognize these divisions:

I. Prologue: The Word Made Flesh (1:1–18)

II. The Signs of the Messiah to the World (1:19–12:50)

III. The Testimony of the Messiah to the Church (13–20)

IV. Epilogue: The Commission of the Disciples (21)

---

3 Donald Guthrie, *New Testament Introduction*, 299.

4 Donald Guthrie, *New Testament Introduction*, 289.

PURPOSE

At the end of Chapter 20, John gives the purpose statement of his Gospel:

> **JOHN PURPOSE STATEMENT:** "But these have been written so that you may believe that Jesus is the Christ, the Son of God; and that believing you may have life in His name" (20:31).

Clement of Alexandria, an early church father, also helps to give some clarity on the purpose of John. Guthrie quotes Clement as saying, "Last of all John perceiving that the bodily or external facts had been set forth in the other Gospels, at the insistence of his disciples and with the inspiration of the Spirit composed a spiritual Gospel."[5] John is writing with an evangelistic purpose. He desires that his readers would believe on Jesus as the Son of God and that by believing have eternal life. Clement testifies that John wrote after the other three Gospels had been composed, recognizing that these Gospels laid out Jesus' life, death, and resurrection in an accurate and reliable manner. John then sought to write a Gospel which had a different focus from the other three. Clement's word is "spiritual," apparently meaning that John wanted to put Jesus' divinity on display. We see this throughout the Gospel, and this will be further explored in the theme of Jesus' divinity.

THEMES

As mentioned in the purpose of the Gospel, Jesus' divinity is on display throughout the book. However, it is not only Jesus' divinity, but the fact that Jesus was both fully God and fully man. This is a key theme that must be examined to understand the nature of the Gospel.

In addition, the role of the Holy Spirit is discussed in John more than any other Gospel. This begins as early as John 3, in Jesus' discussion with Nicodemus. The work of the Holy Spirit is seen throughout the Gospel, giving insight into how we should understand the third Person of the Trinity.

Additionally, John is a key Gospel in helping to determine the timeline of Jesus' ministry. It is because of John that we can pinpoint Jesus' ministry as lasting three years, since Jesus celebrates three Passovers during His ministry. We will examine Jesus' keeping of the feasts and the significance of this during His ministry.

5 Donald Guthrie, *New Testament Introduction*, 285.

Jesus' Divinity

John begins his Gospel with a clear description of the Word of God made flesh. The opening phrase, "In the beginning," points us all the way back to Genesis, and John's statement is clear. The Word, who is Jesus, was in the beginning with the Father. Not only is the Word *with* God, but the Word *is* God. In no uncertain terms, John states that Jesus' nature is divine. This is a foundational text for understanding the Trinity: Three Persons in one Nature. It was through the Son that all things were created. Colossians 1:16–17 states:

> For by Him all things were created, *both* in the heavens and on earth, visible and invisible, whether thrones or dominions or rulers or authorities—all things have been created through Him and for Him. He is before all things, and in Him all things hold together.

There is much discussion about what exactly John means by calling Jesus the Word. *Logos* is the Greek word, and it can convey several different nuances. The central idea is that the Word is the expression of God, not different from God nor just a reflection of God, but the expression of God. There are three distinct Persons of the Trinity, but only one Nature of the Trinity. The nature of the Son, the *Logos*, is the same nature as of the Father, which is the same nature as of the Holy Spirit, but these three are distinct Persons.

A key text to see in regard to the divinity of Jesus is John 5:18: "For this reason therefore the Jews were seeking all the more to kill Him, because He not only was breaking the Sabbath, but also was calling God His own Father, making Himself equal with God."

This is the Pharisees' response to Jesus' healing of the man at Bethesda on the Sabbath. The man was lame, and Jesus healed him and told him to pick up his mat and walk. The Pharisees chided the man for carrying his mat on the Sabbath, a violation of the rule against working on the Sabbath, according to the Pharisees. Jesus answered the Pharisees by saying, "My Father is working until now, and I Myself am working" (John 5:17).

It was based on this statement that the Pharisees thought Jesus was making Himself to be the Son of God and, therefore, equal with God. John continues to elaborate on Jesus' nature after John 5 with the seven I AM statements.

Seven times Jesus makes an I AM statement:

1. John 6:35, 48, 51—"I am the Bread of Life"
2. John 8:12; 9:5—"I am the Light of the World"
3. John 10:7, 9—"I am the Door"

4. John 10:11, 14—"I am the Good Shepherd"
5. John 11:25—"I am the Resurrection and the Life"
6. John 14:6—"I am the Way, the Truth, and the Life"
7. John 15:1—"I am the True Vine"

These statements require careful consideration. Each of these statements serves two functions: 1) to point to Jesus' divinity, equating Jesus with the Father, and 2) to show Jesus' work and ministry. Each of these statements is in a particular context.

"I am the Bread of Life" comes right after Jesus feeds the five thousand in John 6:1–14. The people return to Jesus looking for more food. Jesus tells them to look for the food which leads to eternal life. They point to the manna which God gave the Israelites in the wilderness. Jesus says, "Truly, truly, I say to you, it is not Moses who has given you the bread out of heaven, but it is My Father who gives you the true bread out of heaven. For the bread of God is that which comes down out of heaven, and gives life to the world" (6:32–33). The manna was only a momentary picture, a vanishing representation. Jesus is the Bread of Life. This I AM statement points to the unique role that Jesus has to give eternal life.

We should also notice that John gives a timeframe for this feeding of the five thousand. In John 6:4, the apostle says that the Jewish Passover was near. Immediately afterward, Jesus gives the miracle which points to the truth that He is the Bread of Life. Not only is Jesus showing that He is the true Bread from heaven, but also that He is what the Passover was pointing toward.

This is closely linked with "I am the Light of the World." In John 8:12, Jesus says this is the "light of life." Light and life are linked together in John, as well as in the epistles of John (First, Second, and Third John, and Revelation). Jesus is the true wisdom of God. Jesus points to the fact that those who are hearing Him do not understand. They not only need life but understanding (John 8:14). Jesus reveals God's nature and points to true wisdom from heaven (James 3:17). Just like the Bread of Life, this I AM statement is linked with a Jewish festival, the Feast of Booths (John 7:2). During the Feast of Booths, the Jews would live in temporary shelters to remember the time that God provided for them while they wandered in the wilderness.

"I am the Door" points to the exclusiveness of Jesus. It is only through Jesus that one may obtain this life and light. "I am the Good Shepherd" contrasts Jesus with the false leaders of Israel who were corrupt and wicked.

One might also point to Psalm 23:1, "The LORD is my shepherd." Jesus says "I am the Resurrection and the Life" right before He raises Lazarus from the dead (John 11:25). The raising of Lazarus, a historical fact, was a picture of the future resurrection that believers hope for. Lazarus did not receive a resurrection body, but was only brought back to life, subject to death again at a future time. This amazing miracle by Jesus was meant to illustrate that Jesus has power over death, and it is through Him only that we may have hope of future resurrection, never to be subject to death again.

"I am the Way, the Truth, and the Life" reiterates several of the previous I AM statements. "The Way" is equated with the fact that it is exclusively through Jesus that one obtains salvation, similar to "I am the Door." "The Truth" is linked with Jesus as the true wisdom from above, the Light of the World. "The Life" is linked with Jesus being the Bread of Life.

And finally, "I am the True Vine" points to Jesus not only being the way to salvation, but the means by it. The key idea is abiding with this picture. Jesus is not a key to be used once for salvation. It is in Jesus that Christians continue to abide and live. A branch cut off will wither and perish. It must remain attached to the vine, which is that which gives sustaining life.

All of these statements point to the work and nature of Jesus. Jesus states in John 8:23–24, "You are from below, I am from above; you are of this world, I am not of this world. Therefore, I said to you that you will die in your sins; for unless you believe that I am He, you will die in your sins." Jesus points to the testimony of His Father as well as His own testimony, which He puts on the same level as God the Father's testimony (8:14). Unless they believe that Jesus is God, they will die in their sins.

Also, each time that an I AM statement is used, Jesus points to His divinity. John 8:58 is an important example of this. The Jewish leaders were questioning Jesus, who was claiming to have come from God. Jesus says, "If anyone keeps My word, he will never see death" (8:51). Jesus is speaking about the final death (Rev. 20:14). The Jewish leaders respond, "Surely You are not greater than our father Abraham, who died? The prophets died too; whom do You make Yourself out *to be*?" (John 8:53). They were astonished that Jesus would make a claim of having power over death, since the greatest person that they knew of, Moses, was dead, just like all who came before. Jesus responds, "Truly, Truly, I say to you, before Abraham was born, I am" (8:58). This was a straightforward statement by Jesus in which He is claiming to be God. The Jews understood this, which is why in the next verse they picked up stones to throw at Him. The statement I AM is never applied to anyone in the Old Testament other than God. For Jesus to make this statement, He was clearly and concisely saying that He is God.

John, again and again, points to Jesus' divinity. This is not at the expense of His humanity. John's point is to show that Jesus is both fully God and fully man. The signs of Jesus attest to this. The sayings of Jesus also testify of this. It is not possible to honestly read the Gospel of John and say that Jesus never made the claim to be God. John places this Jesus before the reader, requiring the reader to respond to these clear claims of divinity.

The Holy Spirit

John has more to say about the Holy Spirit than any other Gospel. The Person and role of the Holy Spirit play an essential part in John's writing. The most famous verse in the Bible, John 3:16, is situated within a chapter highlighting the role of the Holy Spirit in salvation. Jesus is speaking with Nicodemus, a Pharisee. Nicodemus authentically seems to desire to know more of Jesus. He calls Jesus a teacher from God. Jesus points Nicodemus to the second birth and says, "Unless one is born again he cannot see the kingdom of God" (3:3). Nicodemus is puzzled by this, and Jesus explains that one must be born of the Spirit. Everyone is born one time, physically. Those who are saved are born again, by the Spirit. Early in his Gospel, John highlights the role of the Spirit in salvation.

John gives a clarifying statement, "But this He spoke of the Spirit, whom those who believed in Him were to receive; for the Spirit was not yet *given*, because Jesus was not yet glorified" (7:39). This paves the way for a greater emphasis on the Spirit in the second half of John's Gospel. The structure of John places great weight on the signs and testimony of Jesus' divinity. However, with Jesus now speaking of His departure (7:33–34), the role of the Holy Spirit is emphasized as the One who will come after Jesus is gone.

In Jesus' farewell discourse (13:31–16:33), He speaks of the Holy Spirit as the One who will come after Jesus has gone. The Holy Spirit, sent by Jesus, is described as "another Helper" who will "be with you forever" (14:16). This Spirit abides with you (14:17). The Spirit will teach you all things (14:26). The Spirit also testifies about Jesus (15:26). The Spirit convicts the world of sin (16:8). It is the Spirit who guides into all truth, and the Spirit glorifies Jesus (16:13–14). The Holy Spirit is not seen as some unknown force or mystical sense. The Holy Spirit is described as a Person with particular role and function in the life of the believer and even of the world in general in terms of conviction of sin. The Father, the Son, and the Spirit work in unison to bring about the will of God, even the salvation of those who believe on Christ.

Timeline of Jesus' Ministry

The Gospel of John is helpful in delineating the timeline of Jesus' ministry. Three different Passover celebrations are mentioned, which shows that Jesus' ministry was over the course of three years. After the wedding in Cana, Jesus goes up to Jerusalem with His disciples for the Passover (2:13). John 6:4 introduces a second Passover and John 11:55 the third. Based on this timeframe we can piece together the timeline for Jesus' three-year ministry.

After the birth of Jesus and the visit of the Magi and the move to Egypt and then back to Israel, the Gospels do not include any additional information until the beginning of His ministry, except for the account in Luke of Jesus at the temple as a boy. Jesus' ministry is inaugurated with His baptism (Matt. 3:13–17; Mark 1:9–11; Luke 3:21–22) and subsequent temptation by Satan (Matt. 4:1–11; Mark 1:12–13; Luke 4:1–13).

It is during the first Passover mentioned that Jesus first cleanses the temple (John 2:13–25). The story of Nicodemus coming to Jesus at night follows this, but it is not certain how far apart the events would have been. Nicodemus calls Jesus Rabbi, which indicates that Jesus' fame and reputation would have begun to spread. John 3:22 says, "After these things," presumably referring to this first Passover celebration and interaction with Nicodemus. It was after this that Jesus and His disciples go into the land of Judea, and John 3:22 mentions that Jesus was baptizing there while John the Baptist was also baptizing.

From this point, it is easiest to break down Jesus' ministry by area. He begins ministering in Judea but then leaves Judea (Matt. 4:12) and moves to Sychar of Samaria (John 4:4–42). This brings about the story of the Samaritan woman at the well. It is telling that this early in Jesus' ministry He does not avoid Samaria but enters it and does ministry there. The Samaritans were hated by the Jews, who saw them as traitors since they were left behind when Israel was sent into exile and intermarried with non-Jews.

After Samaria, Jesus moves to His Galilean ministry (4:43–45) and calls several disciples. During this time He heals the official's son at Capernaum (4:46–54). This brings about a prolonged ministry in Capernaum, where Jesus heals many (Matt. 8:14–17; Mark 1:21–34; Luke 4:31–41). Jesus then leaves the city of Capernaum and ministers throughout Galilee (Matt. 4:23–24, 8:2–4; Mark 1:35–45; Luke 4:38–44, 5:12–16). He then returns to Capernaum and heals a paralytic (Matt. 9:1–8). At this point Matthew is called as a disciple (9:9–13). Matthew 12:1–4 records that it is at this time that Jesus has the first Sabbath controversy, when the Jewish leaders find that His disciples were picking heads of grain and eating them while walking through the grainfields. This, according to the Jewish leaders, was a violation of the Sabbath.

After this, the full twelve disciples are appointed (Mark 3:13–19; Luke 6:12–16). Jesus then goes on a second trip around the Galilee region. At this point the scribes and Pharisees blaspheme Jesus and give their final decision on Him (Matt. 12:22–50). Jesus responds by giving the parables of Matthew 13. Growing opposition to Jesus leads to the rejection of Jesus at Nazareth (Mark 6:1–6). Jesus and the disciples then continue to travel around Galilee (Matt. 14:1–12; Mark 6:6–30; Luke 9:1–10). This culminates in Jesus feeding the five thousand, walking on the water, and also making the statement "I am the Bread of Life" (Matt. 14:13–36; Mark 6:31–56; Luke 9:10–17; John 6:1–21). It is at this point that John says that the second Passover of Jesus' ministry was approaching (6:4).

During this last year of Jesus' life, from the second Passover to the third Passover, the hostility against Jesus escalates (Matt. 15:1–16:12). Jesus spends more time privately instructing the disciples and less time demonstrating miracles (17:14–18:35; Mark 9:14–50; Luke 9:37–50). In addition to going up to Jerusalem for Passover each year, Jesus also went up to Jerusalem for the Feast of Booths (John 7:2–10:21). It is at the Feast of Booths that Jesus makes the statements, "I am the Light of the World" (8:12; 9:5), "I am the Door"(10:7, 9), and "I am the Good Shepherd" (10:11, 14). This not only shows that Jesus reveals the Father and is the exclusive way of salvation, but it is also an indictment against the Pharisees, who were demonstrating growing hostility against Jesus.

Luke 9:51–13:21 records that Jesus ministered throughout the region of Judea around this time. The seventy are sent out (10:1–29), and Jesus gives the parable of the Good Samaritan (10:30–37). Jesus then also goes up to the Feast of Dedication, the third annual feast at which Jews were supposed to go up to Jerusalem (John 10:22). After this feast, John records that Jesus left Judea and went to the region of Perea which is beyond the Jordan River (10:40–42; Luke 13:22–17:10). Jesus gives the parable of the Prodigal Son (15:11–32). On His way back to Jerusalem for the third Passover, Jesus passed between Samaria and Galilee and there healed the ten lepers (Luke 17:11–21). While Jesus was away, Lazarus grows sick and dies. Jesus returns to raise him from the dead after three days (John 11:1–53). This is Jesus' last trip going up to Jerusalem (Matt. 19:1–20:34; Mark 10:1–52; Luke 17:11–19:28; John 11:54). This leads to the final week which is outlined in the chapter on Luke.

Study Questions:

1. What are the seven I AM statements of Jesus? How is each one unique?
2. What is Jesus claiming when He says "I AM"? How did the Jewish leaders respond to this?
3. Why do you think the Holy Spirit is often understood by people as a force rather than as a person? Can you describe some of the characteristics that John attributes to the Holy Spirit? What are the various roles of the Holy Spirit according to John?
4. How many times does Jesus travel around Galilee ministering with His disciples?
5. How does Jesus respond to the growing hostility of the Jewish leaders as His ministry continues?

6

First John

THE EARLY CHURCH attests to the authorship of First John by the apostle John. For further discussion on the distinction between the apostle John and John the Elder, see the chapter on Second John. Irenaeus makes this claim, as well as evidence to support this from Polycarp (a disciple of the apostle John who lived c. AD 69–155), Ignatius (c. AD 35–110), and Papias (c. AD 60–130).[1] What is interesting to note is that John doesn't appeal to his apostolic office in any of his letters. He is content, even though he is an apostle of Jesus who saw and spoke with Jesus, to simply not refer to himself or just to call himself "the elder." For more discussion on the title "the elder," see the chapter on Third John.

What is interesting to note is the simplicity with which John writes. Andreas Köstenberger notes that John only uses 303 different Greek words to write his three letters.[2] We should remember that John was a simple fisherman. He spent the first years of his life mending nets and cleaning fish to sell in the local market. The day that Jesus called John to follow Him, that all changed. John spent three years in the closest contact with Jesus, alongside Peter and James. Even among the twelve disciples, John was in a privileged place. These three years transformed John's life and set him on a trajectory that would lead to his penning five books of the New Testament. John's name is forever emblazoned in the Bible, even though he took care not to even use his own name when writing. John went from being a simple fisherman to speaking with God incarnate to writing five books of the New Testament. John's final book ended a millennium and a half of Scripture being written, from Genesis to Revelation. John, as an author, bears all of these characteristics. His writing is simple, much like you would expect

1 Köstenberger, Kellum, and Quarles, *The Cradle, the Cross, and the Crown*, 784.

2 Köstenberger, Kellum, and Quarles, *The Cradle, the Cross, and the Crown*, 783.

from a fisherman. His writing is also incredibly deep, much like you would expect from someone who has received the greatest revelation. Köstenberger quotes Martin Luther as saying, "I have never read a book written in simpler words than this one [First John], and yet the words are inexpressible."[3]

The date of First John is difficult to pinpoint with certainty. However, it appears that First, Second, and Third John were all written toward the end of John's life, perhaps in the AD 80s or 90s. John grew up in Galilee, and seems to have moved from Palestine to Ephesus subsequent to the start of the Jewish rebellion in AD 66, which led to the temple in Jerusalem being destroyed by Titus.[4] John spent a great deal of time in Ephesus before being banished to the island of Patmos on which he wrote Revelation. The writing of First, Second, and Third John fits well in the period in which John was in Ephesus.

Knowing that John wrote while in Ephesus helps to narrow down the audience somewhat. John does not mention anyone in particular in First John that he is writing to, other than to use general terms such as "children, young men, and fathers." He does write specially to Gaius in Third John and to a general "chosen lady and her children" in Second John. It is possible that all three of John's epistles are directed to churches and individuals around the region of Ephesus, and even more broadly, Asia Minor. The unspecific way in which First John was written seems to indicate that this letter was meant to be widely distributed to many churches. John's tone through his letters is one of love and gentleness toward his intended readers. He has clear commands for them, but he is not writing to browbeat or overwhelm them. As an elderly man who has seen his friends be executed for the gospel, John writes with gravity as well as simplicity.

Structure

First John is an epistle, and as such has a structure like a letter. However, the introduction is different from a typical letter. John does not begin with a salutation or a personal introduction. In a similar manner to the Gospel of John, he immediately begins to write about Jesus, he himself being an eyewitness of the Son of God. John even begins this letter with similar wording to his Gospel. First John 1:1 begins, "What was from the beginning . . ."; John 1:1 begins, "In the beginning . . ." Both introductions speak about the nature of Jesus, being the incarnate Son of God. After the introduction, John's central

3 Köstenberger, Kellum, and Quarles, *The Cradle, the Cross, and the Crown*, 783.

4 Köstenberger, Kellum, and Quarles, *The Cradle, the Cross, and the Crown*, 790.

focus in this first epistle is assurance of salvation. John intertwines many themes and ideas in the body of his letter. The conclusion begins with John's thesis statement (1 John 5:13) and sums up John's exhortation to his readers.

I. Introduction (1:1–4)

II. Body (1:5–5:12)

  a. Assurance and Fellowship (1:5–2:17)

  b. Assurance and Conflict (2:18–4:6)

  c. Assurance and Love (4:7–5:5)

  d. Assurance and the Spirit (5:6–12)

III. Conclusion (5:13–21)

PURPOSE

The main focus of the first epistle of John is assurance of salvation. This is within the context of false believers who have just left the church and caused great problems within the church. John is writing to those who are the true members of the church to encourage them of their salvation. John emphasizes the nature and benefits of this salvation.

> **FIRST JOHN PURPOSE STATEMENT:** To encourage believers in the church to take hold of their assurance of salvation and fellowship with God and the church.

Any description of John's purpose for writing the letter must be linked with his statement in First John 5:13: "These things I have written to you who believe in the name of the Son of God, so that you may know that you have eternal life."

THEMES

The themes of John are linked, and John will often switch from one idea to another because they are so interwoven in his mind. John's intention is to speak of assurance of salvation for true believers. But this is also coupled with John's description of what true love for God looks like, namely, keeping His commands. John also contrasts this with those who are false believers, pretending to love God but, in all reality, seeking to damage the church. John makes use of the metaphor of light and darkness to speak of this throughout this letter. To understand these themes, we will examine John's message of assurance of salvation and contrast this with those who are "walking in darkness."

Many Christians, if not all, struggle with their assurance of salvation at some point in their Christian life. This can be a struggle which comes and goes, or it can be a continual struggle for years. First John is a beautiful little letter that seeks to encourage Christians in this. John is not trying to give false assurance though. He is not trying to make his readers feel okay if they truly are not. John wants true believers to grasp hold of their assurance of salvation.

John makes simple but difficult statements. First John 2:3–4 says, "By this we know that we have come to know Him, if we keep His commandments. The one who says, 'I have come to know Him,' and does not keep His commandments is a liar, and the truth is not in him." Any Christian who reads that will honestly say to himself that he has not perfectly kept the commandments of God. A statement such as this points us to all the times that we have broken the commandments of God. Each of John's statements must be kept in view of the whole book, if we are to properly understand what John is saying.

In contrast to what John says in chapter 2, John clearly says in First John 1:8, "If we say that we have no sin, we are deceiving ourselves and the truth is not in us." John recognizes that everyone is a sinner. So how does this truth fit with the statement that if someone is a Christian, they will keep the commands of God?

First, we should recognize the situation which John is addressing. John has confidence that those he is writing to are saved. He even mentions this in his purpose statement in First John 5:13, "These things I have written to you who believe in the name of the Son of God." This is in contrast to those who were a part of the church but demonstrated that they were not truly Christians. First John 2:18–19 states:

> Children, it is the last hour; and just as you heard that antichrist is coming, even now many antichrists have appeared; from this we know that it is the last hour. They went out from us, but they were not *really* of us; for if they had been of us, they would have remained with us; but *they went out*, so that it would be shown that they all are not of us.

John is writing this letter to a group of believers who have been tested and found to be in the faith. Before he wrote this letter, there were those in the church who pretended to be Christians. They sought their own glory, not Christ's. This is also seen in both Second John with those who are called "deceivers" and in Third John with Diotrephes as the example of an unbeliever who was guided by his own arrogance.

In First John, the apostle uses the term "confidence" three times. First, he speaks of having confidence before God in First John 3:21. Second, he speaks of having confidence on the day of judgment in First John 4:17. Finally, he speaks of having confidence in approaching God in prayer in First John 5:14. The mention of this confidence is surrounded by the things which should assure a believer of their salvation.

The first of these assurances is that a true believer will have a love for the church and for true Christian fellowship. The basis for this assurance is that true Christians have fellowship with God (1 John 1:7). Jesus, being the Advocate for all true believers ensures that fellowship with God cannot be severed. First John 2:1 says, "My little children, I am writing these things to you so that you may not sin. And if anyone sins, we have an Advocate with the Father, Jesus Christ the righteous." Jesus ensures that our fellowship with the Father is never broken. This being the case, all Christians have fellowship with each other as well. First John 2:11 says, "But the one who hates his brother is in the darkness and walks in the darkness." John also warns his readers that to have fellowship with the world is to have enmity toward God. You cannot love the world and love God (2:15–17).

The second assurance of salvation is the conflict between the world and the church. Not only does John give the command not to love the world, but he states that there will be certain conflict between a Christian and the world. A Christian's home is not in the world. This does not mean that a Christian will not enjoy anything that is created. John is not using the term "world" in the sense of the physical world. Christians can and should enjoy the created world. Enjoying good food, building a beautiful house, reading a good book, etc. are all gifts from God. When John uses the term "world" he is not talking about the good things that God gives in the world. He is talking about the world's system, exemplified by the antichrist. John says that the things which characterize the world are:

1. Lusts (2:17)
2. Deception and antichrists (2:18)
3. Denial of the truth (2:22–23)
4. Hatred for Christ's return (2:28)
5. Lawlessness (3:4)
6. Continually practicing sin (3:8)

7. Being of the devil (3:8)
8. Hatred for others (1 John 3:10)
9. Murder and jealousy (3:12)
10. Does not confess Jesus is from God (4:2–3)

The true Christian cannot have fellowship with the world. These are two separate worldviews, two separate systems which will always clash.

The third assurance of salvation is love. Love is misunderstood in today's culture. This is true not only of today's world but also of all time. The world always distorts the true meaning of love. It is John who says, "God is love" (4:8). True Christians understand love. In order to understand and accept the gospel, you must grasp what love is. John defines it: "In this is love, not that we loved God, but that He loved us and sent His Son to be the propitiation for our sins" (4:10). God loved us while we were still His enemies. The world can try to imitate love, but when it comes down to it, the world is only self-seeking. So the world has no motivation, desire, or understanding of love which is self-sacrificing, love which puts someone else's needs above your own, even to the point to self-sacrifice. The world tries to imitate this, but ultimately, even the world's example of sacrifice is selfishly and pridefully motivated. Believing and confessing that Jesus was sent into the world to be the Savior of the world is the first step in understanding true love. True love has its foundation in God. God is the One who defines it. Therefore, any claim of love which is not rooted in God is false. Accepting the truth of God's love allows us to abide in God, finding the definition of love in what God has done for us. If we abide in God, "love is perfected with us." John says that this leads us to "have confidence in the day of judgment" (4:16–17). When a Christian demonstrates true love—love for God and love for their brother—that Christian is assured of their salvation. Only a true Christian can truly love. And our definition of what love is comes from God and is seen in what God has done for us.

The fourth assurance of salvation is from the Spirit. John says that the Spirit testifies that Jesus has come in the flesh (5:6–8). A key passage is First John 2:27, "As for you, the anointing which you received from Him abides in you, and you have no need for anyone to teach you; but as His anointing teaches you about all things, and is true and is not a lie, and just as it has taught you, you abide in Him." Some may take this as a mystical statement indicating that as Christians, we know everything if we just listen to the Spirit. This oftentimes ends up with a Christian trying to figure out whether the Spirit is speaking to them, or they are just speaking to themself. This is not John's intention at all. We must read this in the context.

Just before this verse, John is speaking about those who are trying to deceive the church (1 John 2:26). John is saying that a true Christian cannot be led away into heretical error. The Spirit directs the Christian to the truth of the Word. No true Christian will deny that Jesus is the Son of God and has come in the flesh. In other words, the Spirit directs us into truth. The Spirit will never lead us into a lie. No Christian understands all of Scripture and has perfect doctrine. But the Spirit ensures that no Christian will fall into heresy, denying Christ as Lord.

Study Questions:

1. What are the assurances of salvation in First John?
2. How does John make use of the metaphor of light and darkness to describe believers and unbelievers?
3. How would you define love? Can the world truly show love? Why or why not?
4. What is the relationship between loving God and keeping His commands as explained by John?
5. What does John mean by saying that it is the "last hour" (2:18)?

7

SECOND JOHN

OFTENTIMES, SECOND and Third John are overlooked because of their brevity. However, they have much to offer those who are diligent to study them. Second John begins with a title of the author, "The elder." This is the same for Third John. There has been some debate about who this elder is. This little letter is attributed to the apostle John for good reason, though some try to distinguish the apostle John from John the Elder. This distinction began with Papias who references both the apostle John and John the Elder, though it is not clear that he was trying to distinguish between two different men.[1] Papias lived in the latter half of the first century into the second century, and his remark on the apostle John and John the Elder led several writers after him to believe that the apostle John and John the Elder were two different people. However, it is not clear that this was Papias' intention. It is best to see the apostle John and John the Elder as the same person. The early church attests to the fact that it was the apostle John who wrote Second John, Irenaeus being a key source for this.[2]

The question which arises from this is why did the apostle John call himself the Elder, and not simply John or the apostle John. The fact that he does not mention his own name is similar to the Gospel of John, in which he alludes to himself but only refers to himself as the disciple "whom Jesus loved." As was discussed in the earlier chapter on the Gospel of John, he doesn't mention himself by name, but gives clues in the text to his identity. John is reluctant in all of his writings to give his name, but he is not trying to be completely anonymous, as the author of Hebrews does. Second John has many similarities to both the Gospel of John and

1 Donald Guthrie, *New Testament Introduction*, 881–882.

2 Donald Guthrie, *New Testament Introduction*, 881.

to First John. This evidence all points to the apostle John being the author of Second John.

The date of the book is difficult to pin down. The fact that John uses "The Elder" to refer to himself points to his advanced age at the time of the writing. It is possible that at this point, John may be the only one of the twelve apostles still living. If this was written toward the end of John's life, it is safe to put it in the AD 80s or 90s.

John identifies the recipients of the letter as "the chosen lady and her children, whom I love in the truth" (2 John 1). There is some debate as to whether this was a specific woman and her children to whom John was writing, or a church. John does not mention the woman by name, which is different from Third John, which mentions the recipient by name—Gaius. The fact that the woman's name is left out gives credence to the argument that "the lady and her children" are actually a church or a group of believers that John had a relationship with. This may be similar to John writing to the angels of the seven churches in Revelation 3. The angel, or in this case the woman, are a representative picture of the church itself, the children being those who are members of the church.

Structure

The structure of this short letter is simple. It is clearly a letter with a heading of the author (2 John 1) and a salutation (1–2). John also includes in a greeting, similar to other letters in the New Testament (2 John 3). He begins the body of the letter in verse 4 and carries it through to 11. Verses 12 through 13 are an epilogue, including a statement of greetings from others, the chosen sister (perhaps another church). This is similar to the closing of many New Testament letters such as Romans 16. John indicates in verse 12 that he intends to come and see this church face to face soon.

Purpose

John is writing to encourage this church to continue in their love for each other and to beware of deceivers. John's purpose is not to elaborate on these things, but to give these simple commands before his planned visit to the church.

> **Second John Purpose Statement:** To encourage a local church to continue in love for each other and to beware of deceivers influencing them.

Themes

This little letter does not dedicate space to developing major themes. But that does not mean that Second John does not pull on important and crucial ideas. The phrases and vocabulary that John uses should be seen in light of First John. Just as we saw in the chapter on First John, the simplicity of John's speech should not be mistaken for a lack of depth. For example, John describes the lady's children as "walking in truth" (2 John 4). This is a simple description which contains a deep meaning. To walk in the truth indicates both belief and also an outworking of one's salvation. John, as always, links this together with love. Love for God means walking in His commands. John gives a simple statement that he has found many of the members of the church, if one takes the view that the lady is referring to a local church, holding fast to the gospel truth.

In contrast to those who are walking in the truth, joined together in a local church, John describes deceivers. John describes these deceivers as having "gone out into the world" (2 John 7). What we should notice about verse 7 is that John starts with a plurality and ends with a singular reference. In other words, he says "many" deceivers have gone out into the world. But then he ends by saying that this is "the" deceiver and "the" antichrist. John is saying that anyone who purposefully seeks to deceive the church is part and parcel with the antichrist. Revelation speaks of the antichrist, but John also mentions antichrists (1 John 2:18) who are all seeking to undermine the church through deception.

John links together deception with the antichrist. This follows Jesus' teaching, calling Satan the "father of lies" (John 8:44). Paul even puts liars right next to slave traders and homosexuals (1 Tim. 1:10). We often think in gradations of sins, but we mistakenly think that lying is not a serious offense. Jesus, John, and Paul all point to the gravity of deception. It is an attack on truth itself. John wants to warn this local church to be on the lookout against these wolves. They are defined as being deceivers, which is the central description for both the antichrist and even for Satan himself. Their goal is to turn away the members of the local church from the truth.

This leads John to make a strong statement: if anyone comes to the church and does not bring with them the teaching of the gospel, "do not receive him into *your* house, and do not give him a greeting" (2 John 10). There are many unbelievers that the church should engage with, even giving food and drink to an enemy (Rom. 12:20). In contrast, to those who seek to deceive the church and mislead its members, John says to not even give them a greeting. Do not welcome them or even say hello to them. If you give them a greeting, you "participate in his evil deeds" (2 John 11). This is a strong warning to the church not to be tricked by anyone who does not teach the true gospel. John says that this gospel is the teaching of Christ (2 John 9).

Study Questions:

1. Why would John address his letter to a "chosen lady and her children"? Do you think that John wrote this to a specific lady or to a local church?
2. What does John commend this lady and her children for?
3. What is the warning? And why do you think that John singled out this warning apart from any other instruction he could have given?
4. Why is deception so serious? Is John's warning about lying in general?
5. What is the link between deception and the antichrist?

8

Third John

MANY OF THE ARGUMENTS surrounding the authorship and date of Third John are similar to those of Second John. The early church points to both Second John and Third John as being from the same author.[1] Third John also calls the author "the elder," just as with Second John. This points to the date of the writing as well, putting it toward the end of the apostle John's life. It is interesting to note that he calls himself "the elder." He does not feel the need to call himself "the apostle," thereby appealing to his apostolic authority. He simply wants to be known as "the elder." John's gentle tone comes through all of his writings, but this is always tied together with important commands that John wants his reader to know. John's gentleness cannot be mistaken for complacency or faint-heartedness.

The recipient of Third John is identified. John is writing to "Gaius, whom I love in truth" (3 John 1). This should be taken in a straightforward manner. John wrote to the "chosen lady" in Second John, which has led many to hold the position that he was writing to a local church. However, because he uses a specific name in Third John, we can take this as a particular person whom John was writing to.

The name Gaius is mentioned several other places in the New Testament. Acts 19:29 mentions a Gaius who was seized by an angry mob in Ephesus. Acts 20:4 mentions a Gaius who was from Derbe, probably the same Gaius from Acts 19:29. This Gaius accompanied Paul on a portion of his missionary journey after leaving Ephesus. Paul also mentions Gaius in Romans 16:23, who is hosting Paul in his house. This may still be the same Gaius from Acts, since Paul wrote the letter to the Romans from the same region as mentioned in Acts 19 and 20. First Corinthians 1:14 is the last mention of Gaius, other than Third John. In First Corinthians, Paul

1 Donald Guthrie, *New Testament Introduction*, 881.

says that he baptized Gaius, along with a man named Crispus. This Gaius is linked with the Corinthian church, the same region where Paul wrote his letter to the Romans. So the evidence supports all of these verses as referring to the same Gaius. It is possible, though unprovable, that John is writing to the same Gaius. If John is writing to the same Gaius, this would be about three decades after Gaius' work with Paul.

Structure

The structure is quite similar to Second John. John calls himself "the elder" to introduce the letter (3 John 1). The recipient and salutation come right after (1–4). The body of the letter is verses 5–12. The ending is quite similar to Second John, in which John mentions that he is coming to see Gaius soon. This is a part of the final epilogue which ends the letter (3 John 13–15).

Purpose

Hospitality is the central focus on this short letter. John commends his friend Gaius for being hospitable toward believers, even if they are strangers to Gaius. The warning that is given against Diotrephes also speaks about his lack of hospitality.

> **Third John Purpose Statement:** To commend two brothers for their hospitality and love for the church and to condemn a proud church leader.

Themes

Just as with Second John, this small letter contains many important ideas, even though it is brief. Second John contrasts the truth of the church with those who are deceivers. Third John contrasts true hospitality and generosity of believers with the pride and arrogance of unbelievers. In both cases, John is worried about the impact that these unbelievers will have upon the local church. In Second John, John is worried about deceivers infiltrating the church and leading some astray. In Third John, John is concerned about an arrogant church leader who is causing unnecessary divisions.

John commends both Gaius and also those whom Gaius has been housing. Gaius, as a true follower of Jesus, has demonstrated his love for the church by being hospitable to fellow believers, even those who are strangers to him. John says that Gaius "will do well to send them on their way in a manner worthy of God" (3 John 6). These fellow believers, whom John does not name, are also commended by John. He describes them as having gone out "for the sake of the Name, accepting nothing from the Gentiles" (3 John 7). They deserve support and hospitality because of their sacrifice and dedication to the building up of the church. Paul would be an excellent example of this. Paul mentions a Gaius who showed him hospitality (Romans 16:23), though if John is writing this letter toward the end of his life, this would be at least a decade after Paul was executed by Nero.

John clearly seeks to encourage Gaius with this letter. Oftentimes, it is those like the apostle Paul who are held in great esteem, and rightly so. However, John says that those who are hospitable to these people are "fellow workers with the truth" (3 John 8). Those who support the believers who go out are working alongside them to build up the church and proclaim the gospel. John calls Gaius one of those fellow workers.

John turns his attention to Diotrephes and changes his tone. Diotrephes is described as an arrogant man, one "who loves to be first" (3 John 9). He is also accusing the apostle John with wicked words. It is because of this reason that John is planning on visiting Gaius and also calling out Diotrephes. John points to the fruit of the believer. This teaching is exactly in line with Jesus' words, "You will know them by their fruits" (Matthew 7:16). Gaius demonstrates good fruit, evidencing his love for the church and for Christ. Diotrephes, though in a position of power in the local church, demonstrates only fruit that shows a wicked and arrogant heart. John gives his summary statement in verse 11: "Beloved, do not imitate what is evil, but what is good. The one who does good is of God; the one who does evil has not seen God." It is important to note that in this verse, John stops speaking singularly to Gaius and instead speaks to a group, "beloved." John is speaking to all believers at this point, encouraging us to bear fruit that demonstrates we love God.

In addition, Demitrius is mentioned at the end of the body of the letter. John is giving a good report about him, but it is not clear why John finds it necessary to mention him. Perhaps Demitrius was linked with Diotrephes. Or perhaps Demitrius was someone whom Diotrephes was fighting against. In any case, John speaks well of Demitrius and emphasizes his testimony by saying "you know that our testimony is true" (3 John 12).

John, just as in Second John, desires to see Gaius face to face. This warm letter shows John's love for those who hold fast to the truth. Those who love God evidence their love in their good works. These good works are not a way to earn merit with God. They are only the fruit coming from a heart that desires to please God. John reminds Gaius that "You will know them by their fruits."

Study Questions:

1. What is the central focus of Third John?
2. Why, do you think, John would describe himself as "the elder" rather than as "the apostle"?
3. Why would John mention Demitrius? Why is he mentioned at the end of the letter?
4. What is the relationship between bearing fruit and being "of God" (3 John 11)?
5. Why would John say that "the one who does evil has not seen God" (3 John 11)? How is this idea of seeing God linked with First John?

9

Revelation

THE AUTHOR OF Revelation is the apostle John, who identifies himself in Revelation 1:1. What is interesting is that this is the first time that John does so. He does not identify himself by name in his Gospel, but he does allude to himself in his Gospel. The same happens in First, Second, and Third John. There is some debate, even in the early church, about which John wrote Revelation. Some propose that it was not the apostle John, but another John of church history. For more discussion on this, see the chapter on Second John. There are several other Johns in the New Testament, even including John the Baptist. However, the language fits the apostle John's other writings. There is no need to find another John as the author of Revelation.

John mentions his own name in Revelation 1:1, 4, 9 and at the end of the book in Revelation 22:8. John does not call himself an apostle. In fact, nowhere in the New Testament does John call himself an apostle. It is curious that he mentions his own name in these four instances in Revelation, whereas he does not mention his own name in any of his other writings. The name John was quite common in the first century, but John was well known enough that he did not need to explain who he was to his audience. Instead of taking the title of apostle, which John was, he preferred to refer to himself as a servant (1:1) as well as a brother to those he is addressing (1:9).

The dating of Revelation is much debated. This is tied to one's interpretation of the book as well. Some scholars take the view that the events which are described in John mostly occurred before the destruction of Jerusalem and the Jewish temple by the Romans. These would refer to themselves as Preterists. Preterists will date the book earlier than AD 70 because they propose that the prophecies are about the rebellion and subsequent destruction of the temple in that year, the rebellion beginning in AD 66. Oftentimes, Preterists will point to the temple reference in Revelation 11:1–2:

> Then there was given me a measuring rod like a staff; and someone said, "Get up and measure the temple of God and the altar, and those who worship in it. Leave out the court which is outside the temple and do not measure it, for it has been given to the nations; and they will tread under foot the holy city for forty-two months."

Preterists argue that this temple must be the second temple, built by Zerubbabel and enlarged by Herod the Great. The temple only stood until AD 70. Therefore, the writing of Revelation must be before that time. However, it is possible that Herod's temple was no longer standing, and John was measuring the temple in the vision which will be built. This would also be the case with the temple depicted by Ezekiel 40–48. Ezekiel also measures a temple which was not Solomon's temple, a temple which Ezekiel prophecies will be built in the future. This temple in Revelation 11:2 is said to be in Jerusalem, so it is best to see this as the temple of John's vision which will be built in the city of Jerusalem, not Herod's temple.

Preterists make several other arguments for dating Revelation before AD 70, including the argument that the seven heads of Revelation 17:9–11 are the first seven emperors of Rome, with Nero being the sixth. Revelation 17:10 says that the sixth head/king "is," indicating that he is the king currently reigning. This would mean that Nero was currently reigning when John was writing.

The dating of Revelation is certainly wrapped up with one's interpretation of the book. There are no definite internal indicators as to when John wrote the book. There is a great deal of external witness from the early church stating that John wrote Revelation during the reign of Domitian.[1] Irenaeus is the key witness to this, Irenaeus being a disciple of Polycarp, who was a disciple of the apostle John. Preterist arguments for the early dating of Revelation, while attempting to be true to the text, do not sufficiently address the issue of the date of the book. It is best to see Revelation as being written during the reign of Domitian (c. AD 95).

John wrote the book while he was on Patmos, as described in Revelation 1:9. As the early church testifies, John was exiled to Patmos because of his

---

1 For a detailed examination of this, see Köstenberger, Kellum, and Quarles, *The Cradle, the Cross, and the Crown*, 822–823.

faith. At this point in John's life, he is most likely the last living apostle, the other apostles having been martyred for the faith. John is an old man on a desolate island in exile.

The recipients of Revelation were seven churches in Asia Minor. The book certainly has a broader audience in mind; John is writing to all those who have faith in Christ and are awaiting His return. However, John specifically singles out these seven churches, calling their deeds to attention. These churches are called to stand fast against the wicked world around them, as examples to all those who hope in Christ.

The first church mentioned is Ephesus. This is the central point of John's ministry. Before being banished, John was the pastor of the church at Ephesus, Polycarp taking over after John. Ephesus was a major metropolis in the area, known for the temple of Artemis which was one of the wonders of the ancient world. The church in Ephesus is commended for their perseverance and hatred of false teachers. The emphasis on false teachers points back to Second and Third John. The Ephesian church is castigated for leaving their first love (Rev. 2:4).

While the Ephesian church hated false teachers as well as the "Nicolaitans," several other churches are condemned by John for allowing false teaching into their midst. Pergamum has some members who hold to false teaching which is linked together with Balaam's teaching (2:14). There are also those in the church of Pergamum who hold to the teaching of the Nicolaitans. The church of Thyatira had a prophetess in the church that John says is a Jezebel (2:20). The church of Sardis is condemned for having incomplete work before the Lord. The church of Laodicea is condemned for being lukewarm (3:16). Several of the churches are commanded to repent and turn from their ways back to the Lord.

However, John also commends many things about these churches. Ephesus has persevered and not succumbed to false teaching. They have not grown weary in their struggle against the world. Smyrna is warned that they are about to be persecuted, but John encourages them that those who are faithful to the end will receive the crown of life. The church of Pergamum is said to dwell where Satan's throne is, but they still did not deny Christ's name. An example is given of Antipas who was martyred for his faith. Thyatira is described as having love and faith and service and perseverance. Sardis had only a few people in the church who were truly following Christ. The church of Philadelphia was the most commended because they had not denied Christ's name. They kept Christ's word and

Jesus' promises, "I also will keep you from the hour of testing, that *hour* which is about to come upon the whole world, to test those who dwell on the earth" (3:10).

Throughout this section in which John is addressing these churches, there is a great emphasis on standing firm. The time of testing is here, and a greater time of testing is coming. John consistently reminds the churches of this and tells them to stand fast. This sets up the entire book for the battle between the wicked system of the world and the coming King. The consistent refrain is, "He who has an ear, let him hear what the Spirit says to the churches" (Rev. 3:22). This is meant to wake the church up, encouraging them to be steadfast and pure in their belief.

Structure

The structure of Revelation is highly debated. The structure of a book is always linked together with its purpose and message. Since the meaning and interpretation of Revelation is debated, so is its structure. Köstenberger gives some of the most prominent arguments by scholars as to the structure of the book. I will point some of them out here, each of these being proposed by a different commentator:[2]

Revelation can be seen as arranged into a series of six "sevens" (Collins):

1:1–8	Prologue
1:9–3:22	Seven Messages
4:1–8:5	Seven Seals
8:2–11:19	Seven Trumpets
12:1–15:4	Seven Unnumbered Visions
15:1–16:20	Seven Bowls
17:1–19:10	Babylon Appendix
19:11–21:8	Seven Unnumbered Visions
21:9–22:5	Jerusalem Appendix
22:6–21	Epilogue

2 Köstenberger, Kellum, and Quarles, *The Cradle, the Cross, and the Crown*, 836–839.

Another option is to see Revelation arranged like a chiasm (Lee):

1:1–20: A: Prologue
2:1–3:22: B: Present Situation
4:1–5:14: C: The Fundamental Paradigm
6:1–17: D: Judgment and Defeat of God's Enemies (1)
7:1–17: E: Faithful Believers
8:1–10:11: F: Judgment and Defeat of God's Enemies (2)
11:1–19: G: The False Power of the Beast
12:1–6: H: A Woman
12:7–18: I: Judgment and Defeat of God's Enemies (3)
13:1–18: J: Moment of Decision
14:1–20: J': Moment of Decision
15:1–16:21: I': Judgment and Defeat of God's Enemies (3)
17:1–6: H': A Woman
17:7–18: G': The False Power of the Beast
18:1–24: F': Judgment and Defeat of God's Enemies (2)
19:1–10: E': The Faithful Believers
19:11–21: D': Judgment and Defeat of God's Enemies (1)
20:1–10: C': The Fundamental Paradigm
20:11–22:5: B': Future Situation
22:6–21: A': Epilogue

There are also arguments for a simpler structure of the book such as a threefold division (Walvoord):

I. 1:9–18—Past: "What you have seen" (1:19)

II. 2:1–3:22—Present: "What is"

III. 4:1–22:5—Future: "What will take place"

Putting Revelation into a single structural form proves difficult. There seem to be several structures at work which organize the book. Perhaps the clearest structure of the book are the visions of John. In this way the book would be broken down accordingly:

I. The Prologue (1:1–18)
II. The First Vision: The Church (1:9–3:22)
III. The Second Vision: The Great Tribulation (4:1–16:21)
IV. The Third Vision: The Second Coming of Christ (17:1–21:8)
V. The Fourth Vision: The Eternal State (21:9–22:5)
VI. The Epilogue (22:6–21)

However, each of these proposed structures reflects the interpretation of Revelation. For example, to place Revelation 4:1–16:21 into the structure of the Great Tribulation is already demonstrating a dispensational view of the book as a whole. Therefore, perhaps even more essential than determining the structure is to understand one's interpretive methodology for this book.

Purpose

In several places in Revelation, the apostle John says he has been commanded to write Revelation. Revelation 1:19 is a statement by Jesus to John, "Therefore, write the things which you have seen, and the things which are, and the things which will take place after these things." The same is said in Revelation 1:11, as well as in several places in the second and third chapters. John is obeying the command of Jesus to write this book, recounting what he sees.

John is also writing this to seven churches, as has been mentioned above. The book is directed toward the church, and the purpose is to encourage the church. Eschatology, the study of last things, must always go hand in hand with ecclesiology, the study of the church. Often we become so wrapped up in trying to decipher the book of Revelation, treating it like a codebook, that we forget its present purpose for the church. This revelation is meant to give the church hope, giving a glimpse of the glorious realities which await the Christian when God sets all things right. The book also is meant to wake up all believers to be alert and ready for the coming of Christ. The commands and rebukes given to the seven churches point to this purpose as well.

Revelation Purpose Statement: To reveal the glory of Jesus Christ who is coming back, in order to encourage the church to be steadfast and faithful in a world of wickedness.

Themes

Just as with the structure, the date, and even with the purpose, the lens with which someone interprets Revelation will affect the themes which are seen in the book. I have drawn upon several themes in Revelation, but this list is by no means exhaustive. Throughout church history, there have been many varied interpretations of the book. And this continues today, with current commentaries making specific arguments about how one should understand the book. What we must first understand is that John is not trying to be mysterious or difficult. He is not trying to confuse the reader. John is simply describing what he has seen and been told to write down. The difficulty with understanding the book lies in the content. We can view this as similar to Genesis 1–11. Genesis describes a world that is vastly different than the one in which we live in the 21st century. Genesis describes a worldwide flood, humans who live almost 1,000 years, as well as many other things which we do not currently see today. Just because we haven't experienced these things in our own short lives doesn't mean that they did not exist. In like manner, Revelation describes things we find difficult to comprehend, not the least of which is heaven. John also uses figurative language, using the word "like" many times throughout the book. Revelation 1:10 says that John heard a voice like a trumpet. Jesus' feet are described as being like glowing bronze (1:15). Jesus will come back like a thief in the night (3:3). The creatures of Revelation 4 are described as being like a lion, like an ox, like a man, and like an eagle. The heavens receded like a scroll being rolled up (6:14). The locusts of Revelation 9 are described as being like a scorpion, like a horse, and having hair like a woman's hair and teeth like a lion's teeth. John is using language to describe something that has never been seen before. These creatures of Revelation 9 cannot be compared with anything that is living on the earth today. This raises the question about how we are able to interpret these descriptions at all. Is John saying that at some time in the future these creatures will come upon the earth? Or is this meant to be figurative only? Commentators differ on this. Let me give my own general perspective on the book to help clarify what position I am writing from.

First, I would argue that Revelation is mostly speaking about future events. The churches John was addressing were churches of his time, real churches in Ephesus, Pergamum, etc. But John's visions point to the future, to what has not happened, not even two millennia later. Additionally, it is important to link together the book of Daniel with Revelation, as well as the Olivet Discourse of Jesus. These all are pointing to a future time in which Christ returns.

Additionally, I would see Christ's return as occurring after a literal seven-year tribulation. It is at the end of this tribulation, the likes of which the world has never seen before (Matt. 24:21), that Jesus returns and sets up His kingdom on the earth. Jesus rules for 1,000 years from the throne of David at which point Satan is let loose for a short time. The defeat of Satan and his forces is followed by the Great White Throne judgment, the final judgment of the world. Then the new heavens and the new earth are created. Many Bible scholars disagree on these things. It is important to recognize that no one has a perfect interpretation of what will happen. And the point of Revelation is to provide hope to the church to encourage the church to persevere in faith until the end.

The Revelation of Jesus Christ

The central focus of Revelation is Jesus. In fact, the title is "The Revelation of Jesus Christ" (1:1). The point and culmination is the glory of Jesus, demonstrating Christ's rulership and ultimate authority as the Creator and Redeemer. Jesus' divinity is on full display. One of the greatest attestations of Jesus' divinity is Revelation 1:17–18. Jesus says, "Do not be afraid; I am the first and the last, the living One; and I was dead, and behold, I am alive forevermore, and I have the keys of death and of Hades." Jesus is also described to the churches as "The One who holds the seven stars in His right hand, the One who walks among the seven golden lampstands" (2:1); "The first and the last, who was dead, and has come to life" (2:8); "The One who has the sharp two-edged sword" (2:12); "The Son of God, who has eyes like a flame of fire, and His feet are like burnished bronze" (2:18); "He who has the seven Spirits of God and the seven stars" (3:1); "He who is holy, who is true, who has the key of David, who opens and no one will shut, and who shuts and no one opens" (3:7); and "The Amen, the faithful and true Witness, the Beginning of the creation of God" (3:14). Each of these descriptions points to the glory of the Son of God. Jesus is described as both the First and the Last, a title given only to God, and also the One who was dead and is alive.

Revelation 4 is a description of the throne room of God. Many similarities can be seen with Ezekiel 1 and Isaiah 6. Revelation 5 begins the story of this book. In God's right hand is a book with seven seals. No one in all of heaven and earth could open it except the Lamb (5:5–7). Jesus, the Lamb of God, receives the same praise and worship as He who sits on the throne (5:11–14). The opening of this seven-sealed book in Revelation 6 begins the outpouring of the wrath of God on the earth.

Israel is depicted in Revelation 12 as a woman who gave birth to Jesus, "A male *child*, who is to rule all the nations with a rod of iron; and her child was caught up to God and to His throne" (12:5). But the woman fled from Satan, depicted as a great dragon. It is this dragon who knows "that he has *only* a short time" (12:12). The Lamb stands victorious over all who wage war against God. After the depiction of the rebellion against God and God's wrath being outpoured in the middle of Revelation, Revelation 17:14 points back to the Lamb who is described as overcoming all rebellion. After the destruction of Babylon, the marriage feast of the Lamb is described in Revelation 19:7–10. Jesus is the King of kings and Lord of lords (19:16), coming to pour out the wrath of God upon the world, establishing His kingdom on the earth for 1,000 years (20:2–6). Satan is freed after the 1,000 years and defeated (20:7–10), and the Great White Throne judgment takes place (20:11–15). These latter chapters speak of the throne of God and of the Lamb (22:3). The Lamb speaks the faithful and true words. And it is the Lamb who says, "Behold, I am coming quickly, and My reward *is* with Me, to render to every man according to what he has done. I am the Alpha and the Omega, the first and the last, the beginning and the end" (Rev. 22:12–13). The emphasis of the entire book of Revelation is upon the Lamb who will rule all, giving life to all those who follow Him. This is the true revelation of Jesus Christ in all His glory.

The Wrath of God

What most people think about when they think about Revelation is the wrath of God, all of the judgment which comes upon the world. Truly the description of these judgments is horrific. The wrath of God is exemplified by three sets of seven judgments. The first are the Seal Judgments, which come from the book which God has in His hand, which only the Lamb is worthy to open. The first four of these seals are known as the four horsemen of the apocalypse, which is another term for Revelation. The first is a rider on a white horse who has a bow and a crown and he goes out conquering. The second is a rider on a red horse who takes peace from the earth. The third is a rider on a black horse, who brings famine. The fourth is a rider on an ashen horse whose name is Death, and Hades followed him. Revelation 6:8 says that power was given to these four over a fourth of the earth "to kill with sword and with famine and with pestilence and by the wild beasts of the earth."

The fifth seal revealed the martyrs of Jesus. They are underneath the altar, having been slain because they would not renounce Christ. Their refrain is

"How long, O Lord, holy and true, will You refrain from judging and avenging our blood on those who dwell on the earth?" (6:10). The sixth seals brings a great earthquake. The sun turns black and the moon becomes like blood. Revelation 6:13 says that the stars of the sky fell to the earth. It is statements like this which are difficult to determine. Up until this point, we are able to take everything at face value. But how can we understand the stars falling from the sky? What John is portraying here is difficult to pin down. Elsewhere, Revelation speaks of the dragon sweeping a third of the stars to the earth, the stars speaking of the angels which followed Satan in rebellion (12:4, 9).

The seventh seal brings about silence in heaven for half an hour (8:1). This also brings about the next set of judgments, the Trumpet Judgments. The first of these brings about hail and fire, mixed with blood which is thrown to the earth. The second is "something like a great mountain burning with fire" which is thrown into the sea (Rev. 8:8) resulting in a third of the sea becoming blood. The third is a star which falls from heaven which poisons a third of the rivers of the earth. The fourth is the darkening of a third of the sun, moon, and stars. It is this reference to a third of the stars being darkened that points to a different interpretation for the previous mention of the stars falling from the sky. It is these sorts of details which bring about so many varied interpretations from Bible scholars.

The fifth Trumpet Judgment is a star which falls from heaven. Interestingly, the text says, "I saw a star from heaven which had fallen to the earth; and the key of the bottomless pit was given to him. He opened the bottomless pit" (9:1–2). This is a clear indication that when John speaks about stars, he may, at times, be speaking about angelic or demonic beings. Out of the pit come the locusts who are described as looking like scorpions as well as looking like horses. They also have faces like men, hair like women, and teeth like lions. They are given power to torment unbelievers for five months, such that "In those days men will seek death and will not find it; they will long to die, and death flees from them" (9:6). The sixth Trumpet Judgment is an army of two hundred million horsemen. It is from these last three judgments that a third of all mankind is killed. The seventh trumpet is a declaration that Christ now rules over the kingdom of the world.

The final seven judgments are the Bowl Judgments, beginning in Revelation 16. The first is a judgment which produces loathsome sores on all unbelievers. The second is a judgment against the sea, turning all the sea into blood so that everything living in the sea dies. The third is a judgment against all the rivers and springs of water, turning them all to blood. The fourth judgment is that the sun scorches men with fire. The fifth is that the kingdom of the antichrist becomes darkened so that those living in the kingdom "gnawed their tongues because of pain" (16:10). The sixth is that the Euphrates is dried up, making a way for the gathering of the armies at Armageddon. The seventh judgment is an earthquake such as the world has never seen. This earthquake splits Jerusalem into three parts and the cities of the nations are toppled. No longer are there any islands and the mountains are brought low. In addition, huge hailstones described as being one hundred pounds each fall from heaven.

After all these judgments, Revelation reiterates again and again that the unbelievers do not repent of their blasphemy or their wickedness. The judgments culminate in the full destruction of Babylon and the destruction of the antichrist's army in Armageddon. At this point, Jesus returns and sets up His kingdom on the earth, reigning for 1,000 years. It is after this time that the Great White Throne judgment takes place, which is the final judgment of God. Revelation 20:15 soberly states, "If anyone's name was not found written in the book of life, he was thrown into the lake of fire."

True Worship vs. Idolatry

It is commonly said, "There are only two types of people in the world." Most of the time, this is too bifurcated. But Revelation depicts two types of people in the world, in an absolute sense. There are those who follow God and those who hate God. Every single person on the earth falls into one of those two categories in Revelation. There is no middle ground, no bystanders or spectators. The time of decision has come in Revelation. Those who are wicked are portrayed in many ways. They are ones who blaspheme God and do not repent of their abominable acts. They are the ones who "worship the beast and his image and whoever receives the mark of his name" (14:11). Babylon is also another important figure. Babylon is depicted as a city, which stands as the center point for all human rebellion. This hearkens back to the Tower of Babel in which all of humanity was trying to unite in rebellion against God. This Babylon is the next attempt to do this. And it is also successful, bringing all of humanity's rebellion together, at least until Babylon is destroyed by God (17).

Babylon is led by the beast, known as the antichrist (13:1–10). Revelation 13:8 says, "All who dwell on the earth will worship him, *everyone* whose name has not been written from the foundation of the world in the book of life of the

Lamb who has been slain." The dragon, who is Satan, gives his authority to this beast, to rule the world and make war against the Saints. Revelation 13:11–18 speaks of a second beast who acts on behalf of the first beast, causing all the world to worship the antichrist. He also performs great signs and miracles, even calling down fire from heaven (13:13). It is this beast who institutes the mark, which all are required to have in order to buy or sell. The mark is said to be six hundred and sixty-six (13:18).

In contrast to this idolatry and the wicked world's system, there are those who follow after God, saved and purified by the Lamb. The two witnesses are central to this. Revelation 11 speaks about these two witnesses who preach the gospel, prophesying for 1,260 days. Revelation 11:5 says that if anyone tries to harm them, they are consumed by fire. This protection remains until, at the end of these 1,260 days, the antichrist murders them (Rev. 11:7). Three days after their death, God will raise them up again, taking them up into heaven.

In addition to these two witnesses, there are the 144,000, 12,000 from each of the 12 tribes of Israel. They are sealed and protected throughout the tribulation. They are wholly dedicated to the Lamb (14:1–5). There is also a great multitude of those who follow the Lamb (7:9–17). They are described as coming from every nation and all tribes and peoples and tongues. They are martyred during the tribulation, remaining steadfast in their faith. Revelation 7:17 says, "For the Lamb in the center of the throne will be their shepherd, and will guide them to springs of the water of life; and God will wipe every tear from their eyes."

This stark contrast between those who truly follow God and those who hate God, worshipping idols and profaning the earth, is seen throughout all of Revelation. There are truly only two groups of people in the world, those who love God and those who hate God. Everyone is called to account for this. The just are rewarded based on their faith in Christ. The wicked are punished everlastingly in the second death. John writes at a time of persecution of the early church, but John recognized that the persecution which he was enduring is not to be compared to the persecution against all Christians which will break out on the world, overseen by the ruling antichrist. John's vision points to a time in the future when the only hope is Christ. No diplomacy, no negotiation, and no bargaining will hold back the hatred of those who war against God and His people. But Revelation assures us that their end is destruction. Jesus is the true Ruler, the true Savior. No other name can save. No other king will ultimately rule. All who have this hope in Christ seek to live purely and faithfully for God. John reminds us that this world's system is not our home. We long for a new home in which all is set right. Revelation 22:20–21 is the fitting end of the Bible, awaiting the return of Jesus:

> He who testifies to these things says, "Yes, I am coming quickly." Amen. Come, Lord Jesus. The grace of the Lord Jesus be with all. Amen.

Study Questions:

1. Why do you think that John uses so much description that is difficult to understand in Revelation?
2. Should we take as much in Revelation literally as we can or does the vision of John allow us to see this book as entirely symbolic? If it is symbolic, then what does it symbolize?
3. What is the purpose of Revelation for the church today? Why is this book so necessary for us?
4. Why does John write to seven churches? Are each of these churches meant to symbolize anything or were they just seven churches in Asia Minor whom John wishes to write to?
5. In what ways is the end of Revelation similar to the beginning of Genesis? In other words, how is the end like the beginning?

CLC
PUBLICATIONS
Fort Washington, PA 19034

This book is published by CLC Publications, an outreach of CLC Ministries International. The purpose of CLC is to make evangelical Christian literature available to all nations so that people may come to faith and maturity in the Lord Jesus Christ. We hope this book has been life changing and has enriched your walk with God through the work of the Holy Spirit. If you would like to know more about CLC, we invite you to visit our website:

www.clcusa.org

To learn more about the remarkable story of the founding of CLC International, we encourage you to read

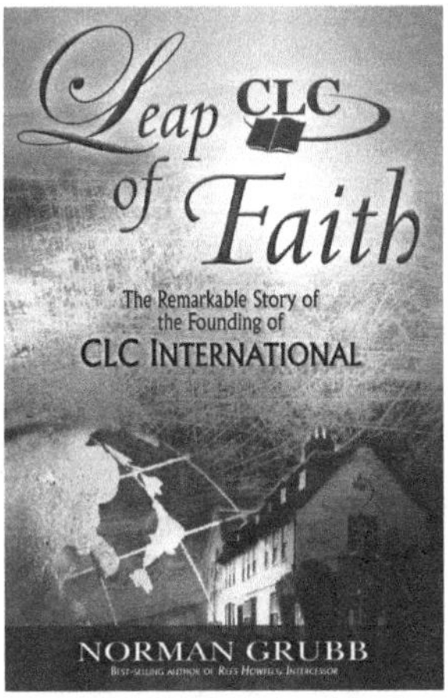

LEAP OF FAITH

Norman Grubb
Paperback
Size 5 1/4 x 8, Pages 248
ISBN: 978-0-87508-650-7
ISBN (*e-book*): 978-1-61958-055-8

Also by

Nathan LeMaster

and published by CLC Publications

Old Testament Survey I

Genesis to Esther

Does the Old Testament matter for the believer today? If all Scripture is inspired by God and profitable for instruction as the book of Second Timothy teaches, then "Yes!" But why does God include chapter after chapter of bewildering laws, land allotments, lists of names, and graphic stories in His divinely inspired Word?

Filled with ancient mysteries and tragedies, the Old Testament both intimidates and intrigues modern readers. Yet the Old Testament contains the foundational tenants of the Christian faith, composing the bulk of the Bible's narrative of redemption. In this first volume of his *Old Testament Survey* (Genesis to Esther), Nathan LeMaster helps the reader navigate these crucial passages, demonstrating the relevancy, intricacy, and intentionality of the Old Testament, reigniting a passion for its study.

Part of the Institute for the Christian Life Series

Paperback
Size 6 x 9, Pages 125
ISBN 978-1-61958-365-8
ISBN (*e-book*) 978-1-61958-377-1